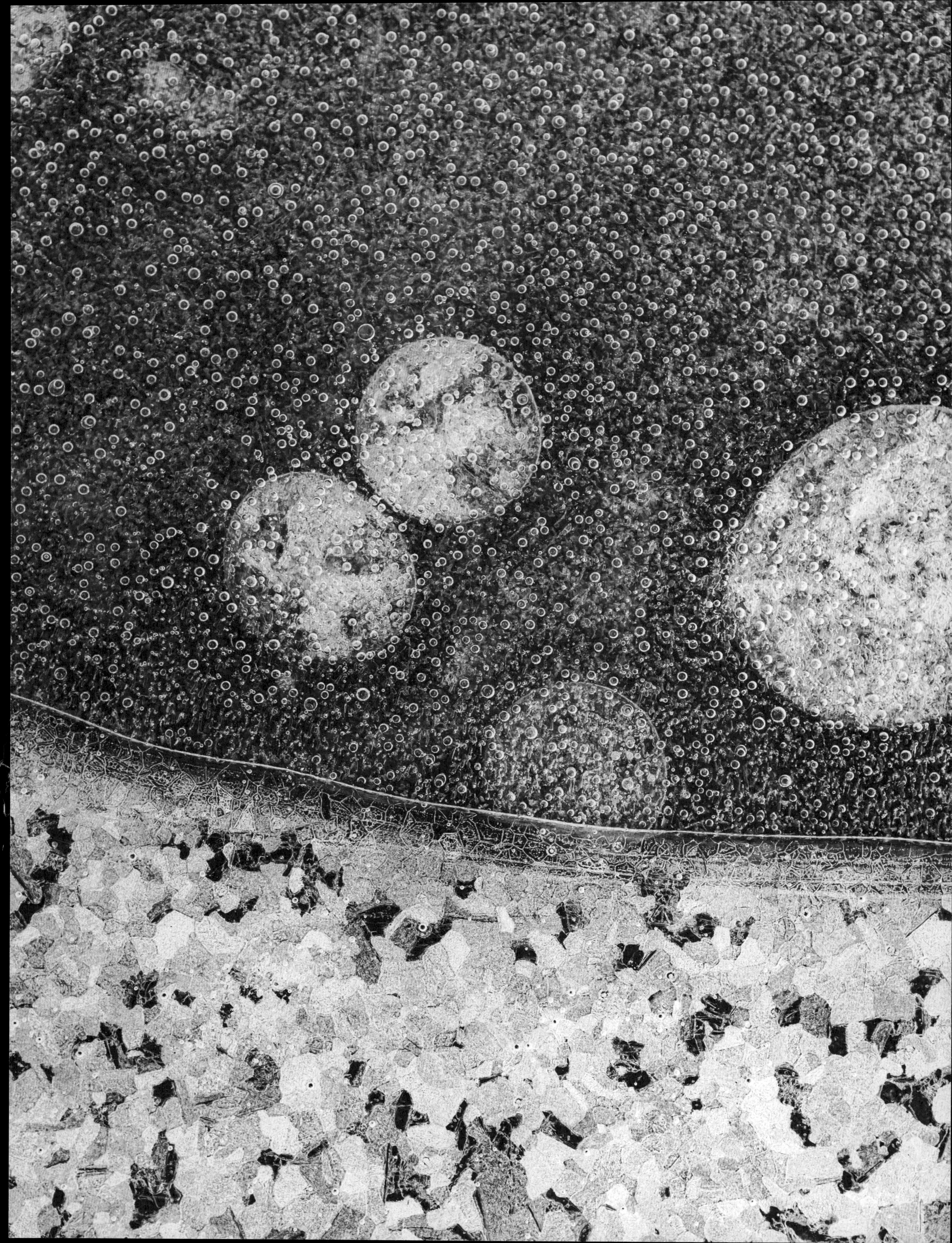

Shelter Cookbook

Leopold Banchini, Lukas Feireiss

Spector Books

This book is published on the occasion of the 17th International Architecture Exhibition—La Biennale di Venezia 2021.

A publication by
Leopold Banchini, Lukas Feireiss

Photography by
Dylan Perrenoud

Cover collage by
Floyd E. Schulze using images from the publications of Lloyd Kahn

Graphic Design by
Floyd E. Schulze / WTHM—Büro für Gestaltung

Printed by
Gutenberg Beuys Feindruckerei GmbH, Langenhagen

Published by
Spector Books Verlagsgesellschaft mbh
Harkortstraße 10
04107 Leipzig
www.spectorbooks.com

Distribution by
Germany, Austria: GVA, Gemeinsame Verlagsauslieferung Göttingen GmbH & Co. KG, www.gva-verlage.de
Switzerland: AVA Verlagsauslieferung AG, www.ava.ch
France, Belgium: Interart Paris, www.interart.fr
UK: Central Books Ltd, www.centralbooks.com
USA, Canada, Central & South America, Africa, Asia: ARTBOOK | D.A.P., www.artbook.com
Australia, New Zealand: Perimeter Distribution, perimeterdistribution.com
Japan: TWELVEBOOKS, twelve-books.com

Second Edition 2025
ISBN 978-3-95905-490-4

There Are Walls That Want to Prowl

Leopold Banchini, Lukas Feireiss

For the 17th International Architecture Exhibition—La Biennale di Venezia 2021, Swiss architect Leopold Banchini and German curator Lukas Feireiss look back on the counterculture of the 1970s. With their installation *There Are Walls That Want to Prowl* and the accompanying *Shelter Cookbook* at hand, they are paying homage to 86-year-old US American publisher and pioneer of green building Lloyd Kahn, who shaped the self-build movement in the USA and worldwide like no other.

There are doors
That want to be free
From their hinges to
Fly with perfect clouds.

There are windows
That want to be
Released from their
Frames to run with
The deer through
Back country meadows

There are walls
That want to prowl
With the mountains
Through the early
Morning dusk.

There are floors
That want to digest
Their furniture into
Flowers and Trees

There are roofs
That want to travel
Gracefully with
The stars through
Circles of Darkness

Richard Brautigan (1935–1984), in: Lloyd Kahn, Bob Easton (Eds.), *Shelter*, Shelter Publications, 1973, pp. 58–59

How will we live together? is the titular question asked by architect and educator Hashim Sarkis, the curator of this year's 17th International Architecture Exhibition—La Biennale di Venezia 2021. With this existential interrogation into the manners of our future living conditions, he makes us reflect not only upon how we will live but also how we want to live together. It is a fundamental question that relates to us on an individual, collective and societal level. It is an equally practical as it is utopian inquiry. It tests our sense of reality as much as it triggers our desire, hope and imagination. It is as much a question as it is a call for action. And it is surely a question with no single but multiple answers. The postponing of the opening of the Biennale due to the worldwide pandemic underlines, in an almost uncanny way, the relevance of the curatorial question regarding our future coexistence. In these few months the world as we know it has changed. But even beyond the current pandemic and its still unforeseeable consequences, the challenges we are facing today and in the decades to come on a global scale are also economic, technological and political, as much as they are social, cultural, legal and ethical. These challenges call for a profound and inclusive dialogue between all actors in society.

Against this backdrop we are, however, not even trying to come up with answers to the open query. Instead we intend to further probe this future-oriented question by turning to experimental models of the past and engaging in a critical dialogue with 85 years old builder, publisher and storyteller Lloyd Kahn. At the heart of this endeavor lies a cross-generational exchange of ideas and inspirations. One that aims to share, analyze and speculate upon the work of Lloyd Kahn—in particular the content of three of his iconic counterculture publications on organic architecture: *Domebook One* (1969), *Domebook 2* (1970) and *Shelter* (1973)—but also upon the influence these works still have on our contemporary architectural practice and imagination.

These nuts-and-bolts compendiums of do-it-yourself building practices, recount stories about alternative dwellings past and present from Iron Age huts to Bedouin tents to Togo's tin-and-thatch houses; nomadic shelters from tipis to mobile homes; and domes, dome cities, and even treehouses. In the path already opened by similar publications at that time, like the *Dome Cookbook* (1967) and the *Whole Earth Catalogue* (1968) for which Kahn served as Shelter editor, his publications aimed to give agency to the people and rapidly became highly successful how-to bibles of owner-built construction. They provided access to alternative educational tools to American counterculture movements that praised ecology and self-sufficiency. In a pre-internet age, these self-made, oversized publications became literally viral. *Shelter* is still in print and has sold an astonishing 300,000 copies to the day. More than just manuals, these best-selling publications also told beautiful tales of the people—women, men and children—who decided to create their households differently, reimagining a way of life in a more conscious relation with the environment, liberated from capitalism and its alienating methods of production.

Beside the poetic beauty and historic value of these documents, many alternative construction methods described in these publications—often ridiculed by modernist architects in the past—are reappearing in more commercial forms today, labeled as eco-friendly. Exactly 50 years later, in a time where the future of our planet seems more uncertain than ever, the various de-growth models presented in these books can be discussed again as serious alternatives to conventional forms of building. In our opinion, the critical reflection of the success and failure of these radically poetic and equally utopian constructions of the past thereby provides an opportunity for highly relevant insights for both present and future. Beyond being a curious finding from the not so far past that capsuled a particular moment in history concerned with living in harmony with the environment, these publications remain highly topical due to their timeless content. Having first reached out to Lloyd Kahn online to express our interest in his work, we eventually traveled together with photographer Dylan Pernoud in early 2020 to the United States and met Kahn and his wife Lesley in their self-built half-acre home in Bolinas, California, where we interviewed him and collected further original material. Installed in the exhibition section in the Arsenale, our project *There Are Walls that Want to Prawl* translates, transforms and extends the conversation we had with Lloyd Kahn into an immersive, multifaceted installation and the accompanying publication at hand. Far from a historical or didactic research, it appears more as a personal quest incorporating different interests and trying to weave unexpected relations and networks by mixing historical documents, contemporary architectural projects, interviews, photo essays and mycological explorations.

Juxtaposing the naturally grown with the artificially constructed, *There Are Walls That Want to Prawl* fosters an alternative vision on how to live together in the future. It has been our explicit intention to create a moment of contemplation, reflection and inspiration with our contribution to the 17th International Architecture Exhibition—La Biennale di Venezia 2021. Rather than solely celebrating our own practices, which we believe to be redundant in the the age of instant access to everyone's entire portfolio on the internet, we deliberately decided to focus on what has been handed down to us from a preceding generation through the person and work of Lloyd Kahn. No nostalgia is involved here, but genuine admiration. We sincerely hope that our personal enthusiasm for him will also spread to the reader. His credits is long due, and if our contribution to the Biennale inspires some of its visitors to pick up one of his publications, and maybe reevaluate one's often preconceived notions of how we live together, it will have more than served its purpose.

Recipes

Leopold Banchini, Lloyd Kahn et al.

The following pages serve as research material. In line with the cross-generational exchange of ideas and inspirations at the heart of this publication, this section confronts building works by Lloyd Kahn himself and from his Shelter publications with contemporary architectural works by Leopold Banchini. In their deliberate juxtaposition wanted as well as unwanted references arise between these diverse projects from around the globe.

Antoine

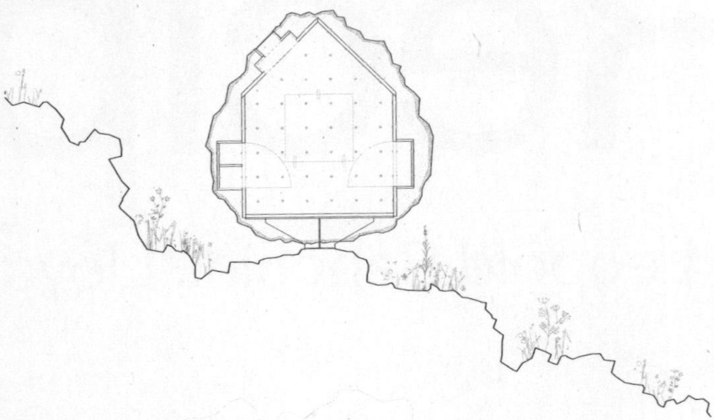

Leopold Banchini and
Daniel Zamarbide

Les Ruinettes, Switzerland, 2016

The novel *Derborence*, describes the massive rock fall that covered the pastures of the valley of Lizerne in 1714. Antoine, the main character, survives seven weeks under the rocks before he manages to reach his village.
Antoine is a tribute to the alpine experience and to the writer. The small wooden cabin, big enough for the life of one man, is hidden inside a projected concrete rock. Referring to the long lasting Swiss tradition of hidden bunkers, the project integrates the highly urbanised landscape of the Alps. Already described by the French philosopher Paul Virilio in 1975, military architecture conducted by principles of camouflage has, for long, fascinated the architects.
Antoine creates an alpine shelter, a precarious "Existenzminimum" somewhat subversive in its use where one can freely enter and hide. It contains the very basic architectural elements—fireplace, bed, table, stool, window—but demands to the visitor some risk taking as the rock hangs literally on the rock fall field.

Text: Daniel Zamarbide

Photography: Dylan Perrenoud

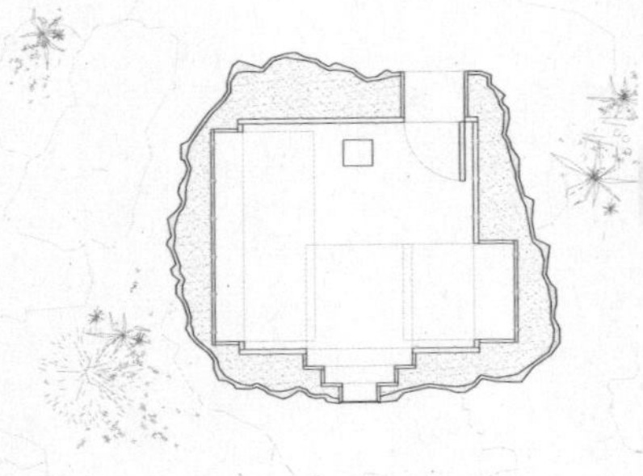

Bedouin Tent

BEDOUIN

Text and drawings by Dale McLeod

THE BLACK TENT

The Bedouin people of the Arabian desert–the Rub' al-Khali or "Empty Quarter"–are primarily nomadic shepherds. This culture, like that of the Hopi Indians has evolved over thousands of years to meet harsh environmental conditions with minimal resources. Sheep and goats are the Bedouins' main source of livelihood, and it is the sparse grazing that causes them to move frequently from place to place.

The tent is a simple, adaptable system. The main structure is a roof rectangle made of woven goat's hair and/or sheep's wool. Together with poles and ropes it acts as a kind of space-frame on which are pinned two long narrow exterior curtains (*ruaq*) and one or more interior curtains (*qata*). Generally the exterior curtains enclose the sides and the interior curtain(s) divide the tent into men's and women's quarters; however in practice an infinite number of enclosures can be generated by hanging the curtains out onto the long tent ropes.

All of these pieces are made up of narrow woven strips—the roof of the tent is known by the name of the goat's hair strips (*filjan*). Generally the strips are purchased in town and sewn together; however the women of the household usually can and do spin and weave this material. The women are responsible for the ongoing maintenance of the tent.

The prosperity of the household is reflected in the length and corresponding number of poles in the roof, and in the decoration of the dividing curtains; a shiekh might have a four-pole tent with elaborate curtains.

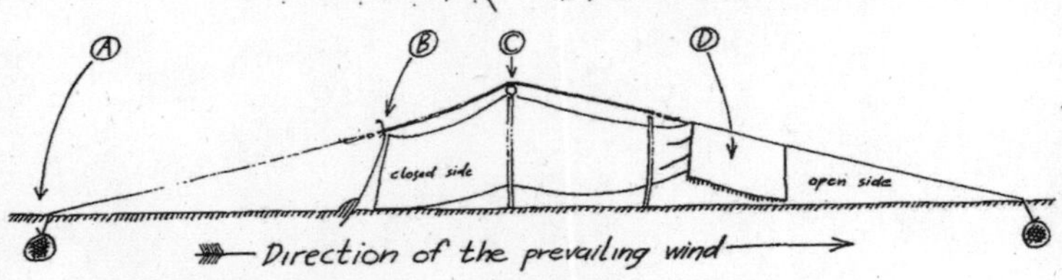

A. BURIED BUSH. method of anchoring tent in sand.
B. EXTERIOR CURTAIN. pinned to the tent roof & buried in the sand on the windward side.
C. CARVED PIECE OF WOOD. articulates tent pole with the tent fabric, sausage-shaped, it is fastened to the fabric.
D. FANCY END OF THE INTERIOR CURTAIN. identifies the front.

Khillal (Pin)

Traditional woven designs on the dividing curtain, QATA, of a well-to-do man's tent. note seams.

METHOD OF TYING ROPES TO TENT ROOF

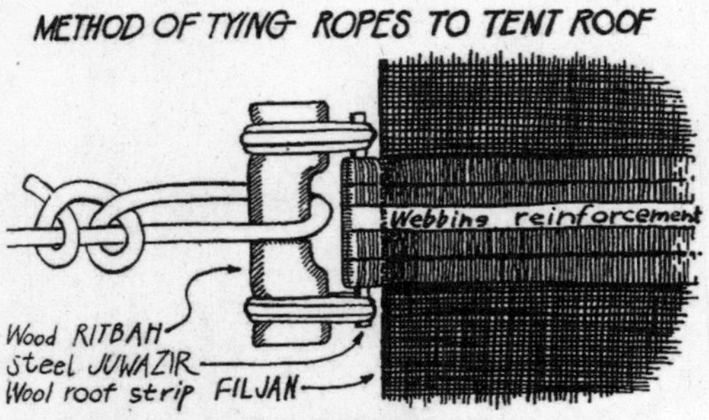

BLACK COFFEE

Bedouin society contained many examples of convention-turned-ritual. Traditionally, a traveller in the desert could always claim three days hospitality in a Bedouin tent, the only refuge there was in a thousand-mile wilderness.

When guests made their appearance it was the duty of the men of the household to prepare coffee. The implements and fuel for the fire were always set out in or near the men's quarters. Coffee making involved first roasting the beans in a long-handled pan and then allowing them to cool in a special box. After the beans were roasted they were pounded in a heavy mortar, then brewed with cardamom in three successive pots. All this took time–it was a getting-to-know-you period. When the taste was satisfactory, the man handed the pot to his eldest son. Holding the small cups in a stack on his wrist the boy poured, just so, a small amount and offered it to the most important guest first. When each guest had drunk as much as he wanted he inverted the cup in a certain way to signify, "enough".

The Bedouins are representative of a diffuse culture that has existed for thousands of years in an area including parts of Asia Minor, Eastern Europe and North Africa. Weaving, and especially rug weaving was brought to an extremely high level by these people before the familiar disintegration-through-contact-with-industrial-civilization set in. I read in a book about carpets that the emmissary from the Belgian court to a certain Persian prince remarked to his king that he had been the first man in history to have trod on the carpets of that palace in boots. When I was a kid in Arabia, during an era which I think of as the million-barrel a day period, the Americans were in the habit of referring to Arab workers in general as "the coolies", and were accustomed to being addressed as "sahib". Now the desert is criscrossed with roads and pipelines and the paraphernalia of American civilization. Soon the Bedouins will be gone....

...I hope you can use my drawings. I'm trying to do a few on the marsh Arabs of Iraq, also. The best book I know on the subject of the Bedouins is The Arab of the Desert, by H.R.P. Dickson (London: Hodder & Stoughton, 1957).

Dale McLeod

Bedouin Population

Arabian Peninsula, North Africa
Since 14th Century

One of the earliest forms of shelter, the tent, is associated with wanderers and nomads. It became a necessary equipment for tribes that needed shelter that was required to be set up and broken down quickly. Although nomadism was prevalent throughout the world it became synonymous with the Bedouin tribes of the Arabian Peninsula. One thing all of the different tribes in this vast geographical region had in common was the Bedouin tent. The tents not only served as a shelter from the harsh desert conditions but also provided space for engaging and hosting guests. The Bedouins were renowned for their hospitality. For travelers in the desert spotting that all too familiar silhouette of a temporary Bedouin village was like to sighting a desert oasis.

Publication: *Shelter*, p. 13

Image: Camp in the Sahara near the Atlas Mountains (Early 19th century)

Bab al Bahrain Pavilion

Leopold Banchini and Noura Al Sayeh Manama

Bahrain, 2012

The Bab al Bahrain pavilion is a temporary public project aiming to open a civil debate on the theme of public space. In addition to lectures, movie screenings, public interviews and workshops, the space is the venue for an exhibition displaying the final entries of the open idea competition for the future of Bab Al Bahrain. It also serves as an open forum for debate, addressing the role of public spaces in the Arab World and Bahrain in particular. One of the few existing public spaces in Manama, the Bab al Bahrain square has been progressively turned into a roundabout almost only dedicated to car traffic. Still, due to its historical importance and its centrality within the island, it holds the potential to become a lively urban public square. Located at the entrance of the Suq it has the advantage of belonging to a tight urban structure which still benefits from a natural pedestrian network. Once located a stone's throw away from the sea, it is today physically separated from it due to the land reclamation projects which have eaten the sea since the 1950s. Considering the recent political events that have taken place across the region, the project seeks to question what a contemporary public space in the Arab World could look like. Climitized malls have now become the main meeting point for locals, leaving the narrow streets of the city center almost only occupied by foreign cheap labor. New developments around the country have encour- aged urban sprawl and privileged cars over pedestrian movements, abandoning most public space to private owner or private transportation means. Recent protests gathering on the Pearl Round-about, a motorway crossing on the outskirt of the city, where only one example of these changes. Built for a couple weeks only, the Bab Al Bahrain pavilion seek to reinstate a strong sense of place and redefine the square as a representative space within Bahrain. The pavilion temporary transforms the central square into a new common space, acting as a 1 to 1 mock-up to open the debate about the future of the place. The light translucent shading fabric covering the entire area modifies the user's perception of the now enclosed space and changes its climatic conditions. Using silver reflective thermal screen, a low-tech technology used for green houses, and the existing fountain evaporation process, it creates a welcoming microclimate. Under the fabric, the traffic is heavily reduced, allowing the public to reclaim the streets and gather for all sorts of activities. Large tables, built in a local workshop, are the only urban furniture added to the existing square. They accommodate competition results and architectural models as well as debate, picnics, games and informal meetings.

Text: Noura Al Sayeh
Photography: Eman Ali

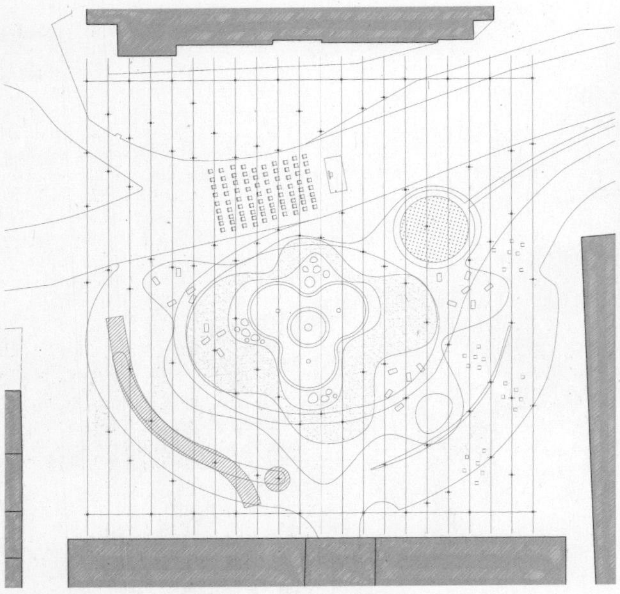

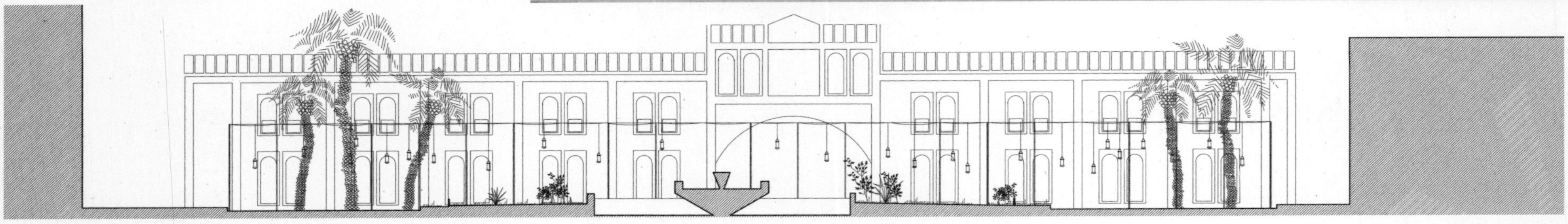

Al Naseej Textile Factory

Leopold Banchini

Bani Jamrah, Bahrain, 2020

The Al Naseef Textile Factory is a textile weaving facility and social space for the local craftspeople of Bani Jamra. It is a component of a broader effort by the Bahrain Authority for Culture and Antiquities aimed at redefining and reinvigorating traditional crafts and industries across Bahrain.
A tight grid of columns and beams is applied to the site as both an organising principle and reference to the significance of the grid in Islamic architecture and culture. The resulting building form is a low and quiet gridded street elevation stretching the entire boundary of the site.
Internally, however, the structure gains figuration derived from the below grade pits in which the weavers sit whilst operating the timber loom. To this end, spaces for both the production of tapestries and weavings as well as social exchange are clearly defined through a series of precise excavations below the finished floor level of the building. Date palms, ponds and cast terrazzo fountains are placed throughout the interior of the project to further break down the rigidity of the gridded timber structure. Composed of regionally available Meranti timber, locally produced terrazzo, aluminium, and Areesh panelling—the construction of the building relies upon and celebrates local construction and craft traditions.

Text: Tobias Beale

Photography: Michiel De Cleene, Leopold Banchini Architects

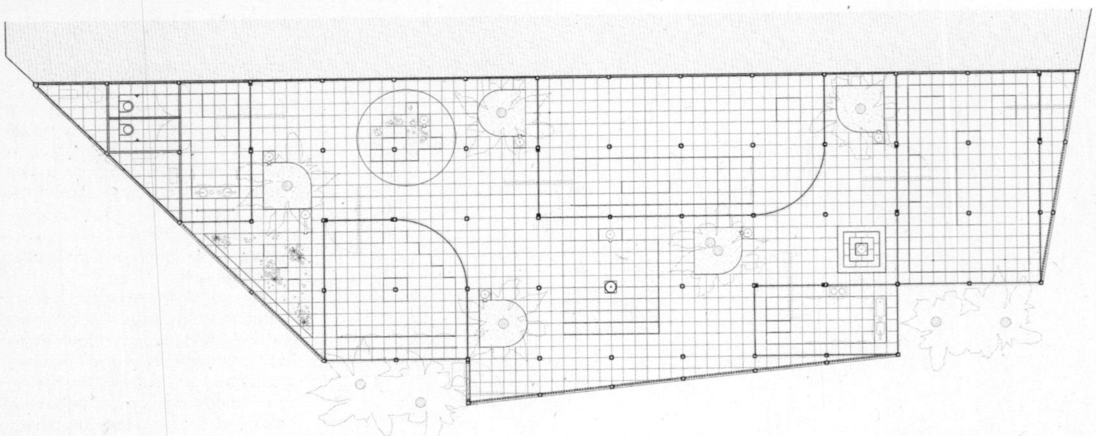

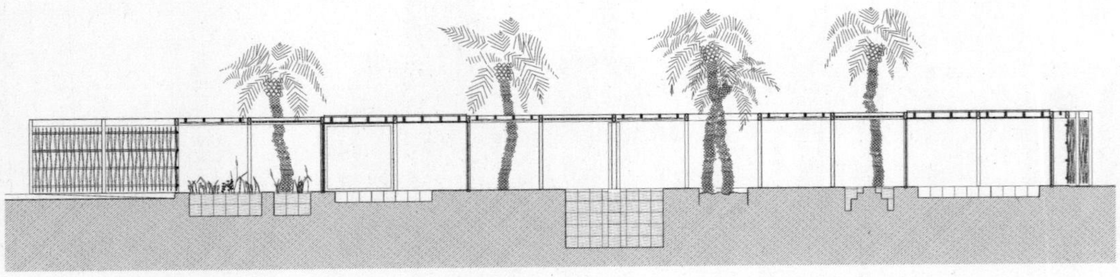

Val Agnoli Tower

TOWER FOLLOWS SHAPE OF WINDSWEPT TREES.

VAL AGNOLI

Val Agnoli is an architect and a master builder, a rare combination in these specialized times. He has built gracefully curved, sculptural houses, as well as simple buildings, and designs for other people as well as himself. His latest project is a simple rectilinear house built of used 4x4's, 2" tongue and groove siding, and asphalt tab shingles.

Lloyd: One thing that interests me is that you're going from curves, very sculptural curves, and now into something much simpler. Is it because you're just moving around trying different things?

Val: I don't know. You feel like you can get almost as much done with straight lines. This thing here, I'm building this way because I want a simple tranquil building. And it's kind of surprising to see how much you can do with just a square little house, you know. Well, little things, like the way this drops down here. I mean, it's not relying on circular forms to give it its value. But I think I'd like to do a wild, a really wild building again. Yeah, really. I mean completely.

Well, how about your own house?

Well, that's a conservative building. It's just an A-frame turned around into elliptical form.

How long did it take you to build?

Not too long. Year and a half, maybe. That was a real ego trip, you know, it was being forced into a role of what I could do as a designer. It was a pretentious move. Had to show your stuff, you know. And it had to be realistic enough so that it was still worth some money when it was done.

How long ago did you do that?

Four years, five years ago.

And the tower came after that?

Yes.

The guy who built the tower, was he meticulous?

Yes. Super, super. And that's what influenced me a lot in the building of it, the design of it was loose. A lot more perforations, a lot more overhang, a lot more balcony, in and out. More transparent. Then as we became closer and closer working on it, we became real buddies, and I picked up on a lot of his vibes, a lot of his direction because I wanted to please him and I respected him. He's a very smart fellow. The trouble is, we ended up making the building tougher and harder and stronger and more fortress-like. Lost all the easy parts to look at, you know. And consequently I felt, personally, I was – at the end of that building I was a fucking paranoic wreck. You know, I was thinking the way he was thinking. And I really got angry with myself for being psyched out that way.

I think that's a transition, just from going around talking to experienced builders, doing complex things then getting back into simple things. Maybe you go back and forth.

You need a taste for adventure, you know. And challenge. It's as exciting as hell. I mean you can hardly catch your breath sometimes when you're fooling around with a real wild design. You don't know what the hell's happening. Like an animal in new territory. It's real intense and exciting. But all of a sudden you say, what the hell am I doing here?

How did you begin building? Your family?

Yeah, my father is a carpenter in New England. Cape Cod houses. Formula houses.

Have you been a boat builder, too?

Yes, but not a real first-class boat builder like... I could build a Monterey hull, I guess, but I haven't. I've been fooling around with rudimentary stuff.

How long have you been housebuilding?

Long time. I guess I built my first house when I was 18. Then I left that to go to school and got an architecture degree. I was also working on big projects like bridges over the Connecticut River. Working as a carpenter. And the St. Lawrence Seaway. When I got to the St. Lawrence Seaway, I decided it was so impersonal and so tough, to can it and go to school. I went to college very late and I had enough practical experience where it really held me back in design. I wasn't able to be naive about lines. I knew what the hell was going to happen when I tried to build it, so I really had to fight against my better judgment.

Bob says you should never draw anything unless you've picked it up. You should never draw any kind of piece of wood unless you know what it feels like.

That's what the enemy of architecture is. It's always been its weakest point, is that it uses paper. And that's its strongest point, too. Because if you stay right here, you can't – and you have a pile of lumber – you just can't visualize that. The pile of lumber will drag. The lumber drags and the gravity drags you back down to reality and you can't soar. So an architect is an unrealistic guy who rises up, then he gets pulled down two pegs by the guy who has to build it, but you're still pretty high up in the air when you finish. The dome...it's a beautiful technical thing. But it's so absolute, so strong, that – Jesus, as a western culture, we don't need any more of this rigid philosophy or manifested form to keep reminding us.

Right, because once you start with it, you're locked in.

Soleri and Fuller are geniuses but the motherfuckers are pushing us right into a locked-in system.

It strikes me often that their kind of thinking is an aristocratic fascism. They're both from very wealthy families, they think in terms of one man laying it all out.

Not once did these guys ever conceive of the fact that maybe you can't live in a fucking hole in the ground or domed city. Maybe what they need to do is walk out into the middle of that field to be sane and valid again. I heard Fuller speak about 15 years ago and he made so much sense he frightened the shit out of me. I don't know why. Everything he said was yeah, yeah, right, and that's true, that's true. But he frightens me, I don't know why.

Well, I listened because I had no education and I had never heard the stuff he was talking about before.

Well, when you talk about a family, a residence, a place – it's the only place that a man can go to have some peace and quiet, in his own little space when he slides that door shut, you know. And that shouldn't be the epitome of rigidity and ... I mean, just this thing over the top of you, you know, this network over the top of you, this grid...it's just as bad or worse, in fact, than the old grid they laid on cities. That was a controlled mania and that's what I like about Boston so much, are all of those fucked-up streets going everywhere.

I thought of that in great preference to Soleri's ideas. You know, just let the city grow, unmanaged, and come back 200 years later and dig up the streets for the underground systems but don't have one man lay it out all ahead of time.

Tokyo is that way, too. Tokyo developed out of a feudal city and so streets are going around this way and there's no grid. They don't all go to the center obviously like Washington or Paris. And that's why it's so hard to get around, but that's why Japanese streets are so beautiful....

I went to this shelter conference in September in L.A. and Soleri was the feature lecturer. The Barrio Planners who were the people from that area in L.A. gave a talk and hardly anybody went to hear them. And one guy got up with an eyepatch, great big guy, Chicano, and said "Who is this Poblari," ah, you know, he says "Who says we should live in these anthills? What is all this dome stuff? I want a house with a yard with a barbecue and a fence around it, and who is this guy who says we should live like this." And of course, nobody was listening to him.

No, because there's no percentages in listening to somebody like that. There is, though, in kneeling before the shrine and nodding to the fellow next to you, "Isn't this great." Well, I don't know. I envision Fuller getting to the moon and putting a dome completely around it. I think that's where his head is. It's religion.

Yeah, that's true. Conceptualization is the thing we've been talking about, the difference between the concept and the reality, and that's the white man's way of doing things, it seems. You get this idea and you don't go out building a house from the materials you have to work with or the site, you go out from an idea. You jam everything into this preconception and, you know...

Jesus Christ, I just remembered. One of our projects in school at Oklahoma with Bruce Goff was – the client had so many thousand railroad ties and this was beginning design and he wanted you to utilize those in the design. And I had just come from working on the St. Lawrence Seaway (laughs) so I ripped them all into 2 by 4's and laminated them together. He was so fucking heartbroken. I said I'm not going to work with those fucking railroad ties. I made it conform to something I knew how to use...

Houses being built now are way too big, too hard to heat, use too much materials.

Sure, that man can do what he's going to do in a third of that area with a roof that leaks a little bit. It doesn't make any difference, water doesn't hurt. If this roof leaks, in this house, it really doesn't make that much difference, a little bit, you know. A lot, of course, and it starts dry rotting. So you gotta be able to live with that little bit of nature coming in on you. And we can't do it. Westerners can't do it.

In California you need so much less space, you can live half outdoors.

You could use planting. For example, you can have an intermediate zone that's planting and kind of like a Eucalyptus trellis with something on it... much of the time you could use that as a building. Like this kitchen. What I want to do is let this kitchen – the breeze is down here. I want to flow out here like the same floorplan, so you can have a table out here and you could sit here and eat, peel vegetables under this kind of shade here...And when the weather gets bad you abandon this outdoor stuff and you come into a small tight space and you get on each other's nerves. But at least the guy and his wife who are going to build it can afford to build the goddamned thing. They don't have to go into debt and ruin their whole lives to pay for the crappy house. So this is too big. This is 600 square feet.

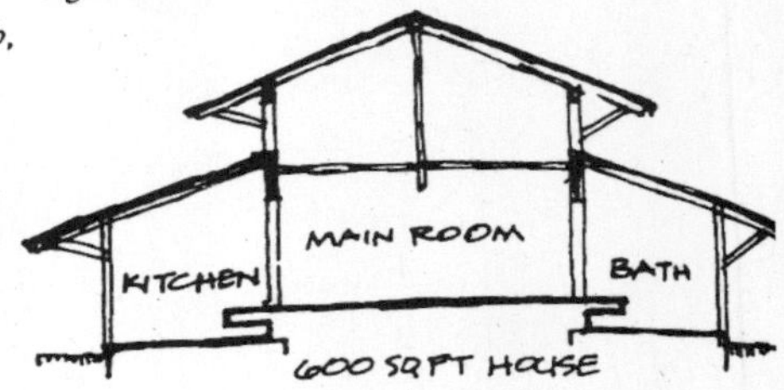

Val then showed me the kitchen, which is a corner of the house with concrete slab floor. (Rest of the house is wood floor, and you step down into the kitchen.) He's going to put 1x1 duckboards over the concrete. He'll be able to hose it out. For cooking he'll build a charcoal fire outside and bring it in for cooking after coals are glowing. I asked him about wood or charcoal cooking on hot days.

You know, I have a great aunt who lives in Italy in the Alps and she has what they call a *fasces.* You know the sign for the Fascist movement in Italy was a band of little twigs bound together. It's called a *fasces.* They'd go into the woods and pick up the droppings from all the trees and they have them in the kitchen, about that long, little twigs. And she has a little cast-iron stove there but it's shallow. It doesn't have a deep fire box. Takes the thing off, breaks a couple in there, lights it and puts a pan right on it. She doesn't build a big fire, you know, just a little fire like that and it's done.

...like a eucalyptus trellis with something on it...much of the time you could use that as a building...so you can have a table out here and you could sit here and eat, peel vegetables under this kind of shade here...

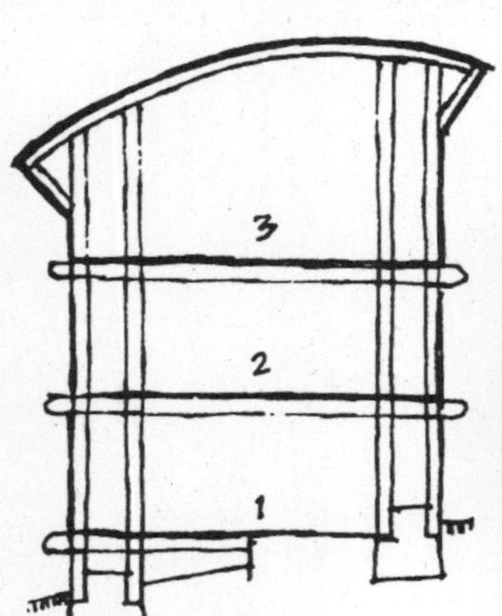

CROSS SECTION

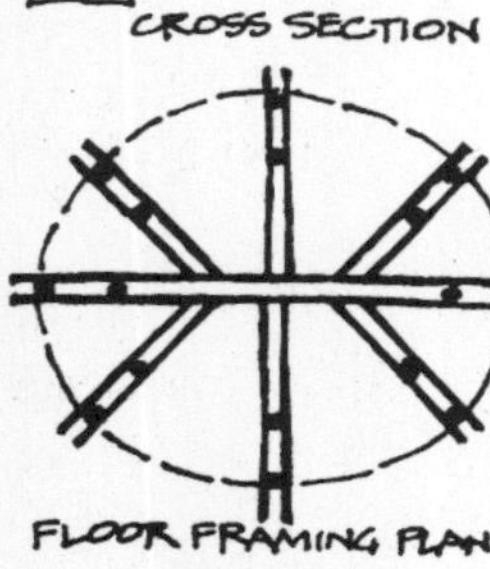

FLOOR FRAMING PLAN
TOWER

Val Agnoli

Stinson Beach, California, USA, 1970

Val Agnoli is what Lloyd Kahn described as "that unusual combination of creative architect and master builder." This unique tower house was designed by Agnoli and built in the 1970's with intricate attention to detail. Magnificent use of wood located in the middle of a tree studded knoll with views of the Pacific Ocean and just steps to the mountain trails. The all wooden tower serves as a reminder of our connection to the physical world in an era where virtual reality has crept into almost every facet of day-to-day life.

Publication: *Shelter*, p. 154

Photography: Dylan Perrenoud

Monte Verita

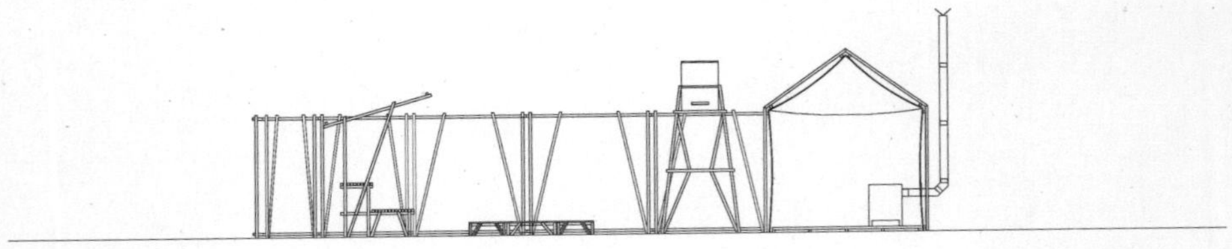

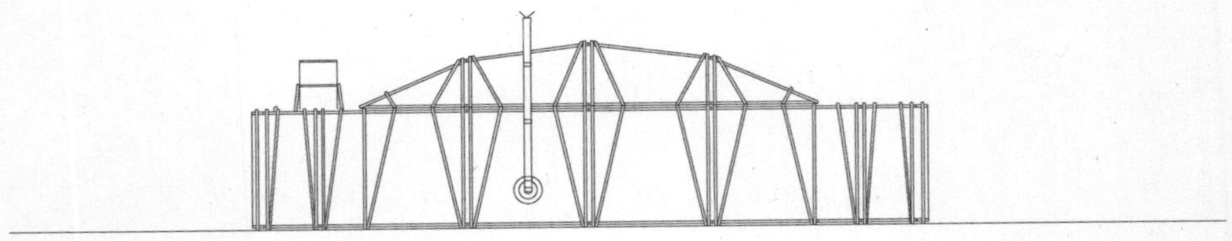

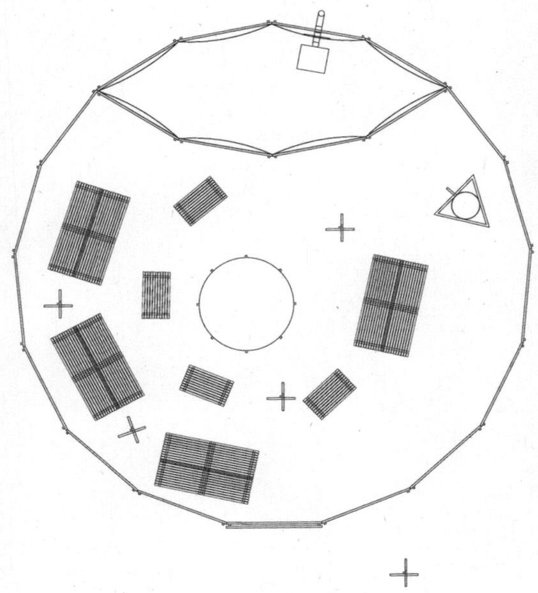

Leopold Banchini and
Daniel Zamarbide

Ticino, Switzerland, 2015

Peut-on être révolutionnaire et aimer les fleurs? (Can one be a revolutionary and love flowers?), written and directed by Dorothée Thébert and Filippo Filliger is a theatre play retracing, in a documentary and yet very free manner, the intense history of the Monte Verità community where Rudolf Steiner, Rudolf Laban, Herman Hesse, Otto Gros, and many other creative and intellectual figures gathered to experiment new forms of living.
The scenography of the play proposes another community, one of simple and functional objects, supporting the activities and movements of the group. Benches, stools, shower, partitions, canopies, bleachers, standing lamps compose an elemental and direct aesthetic. Pine wood studs and natural wool felt referring to Josef Beuys's survival obsession are the main construction materials. The temporary theatre is an itinerary settlement moving with the comedian from town to town. Its details and assembling are conceived to be dismantled and stored easily; architecture at its minimum. A sweat lodge built out of the same materials encourage the visitors and the actors to dress down and celebrate a moment of utopian gathering.

Text: Daniel Zamarbide

Photography: Dorothée Thébert & Leopold Banchini Architects

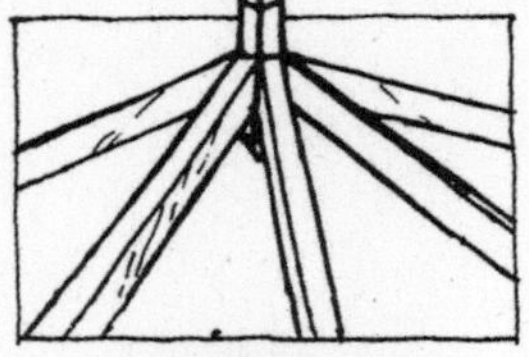

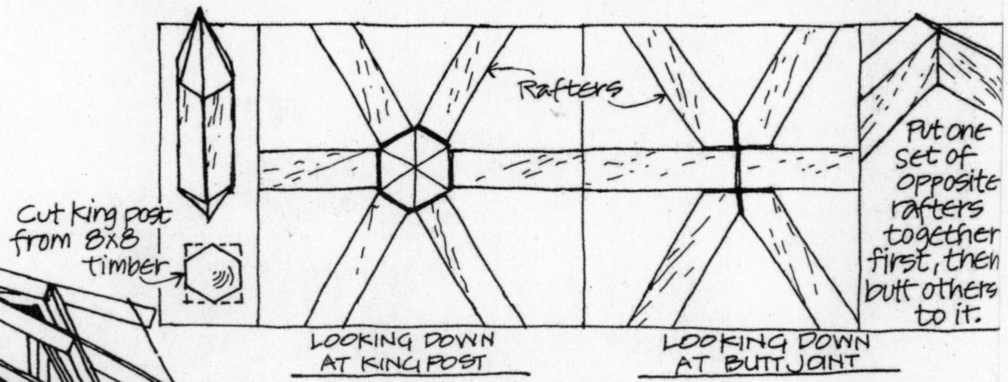

Rafters at Ridge point – 2 ways to frame.

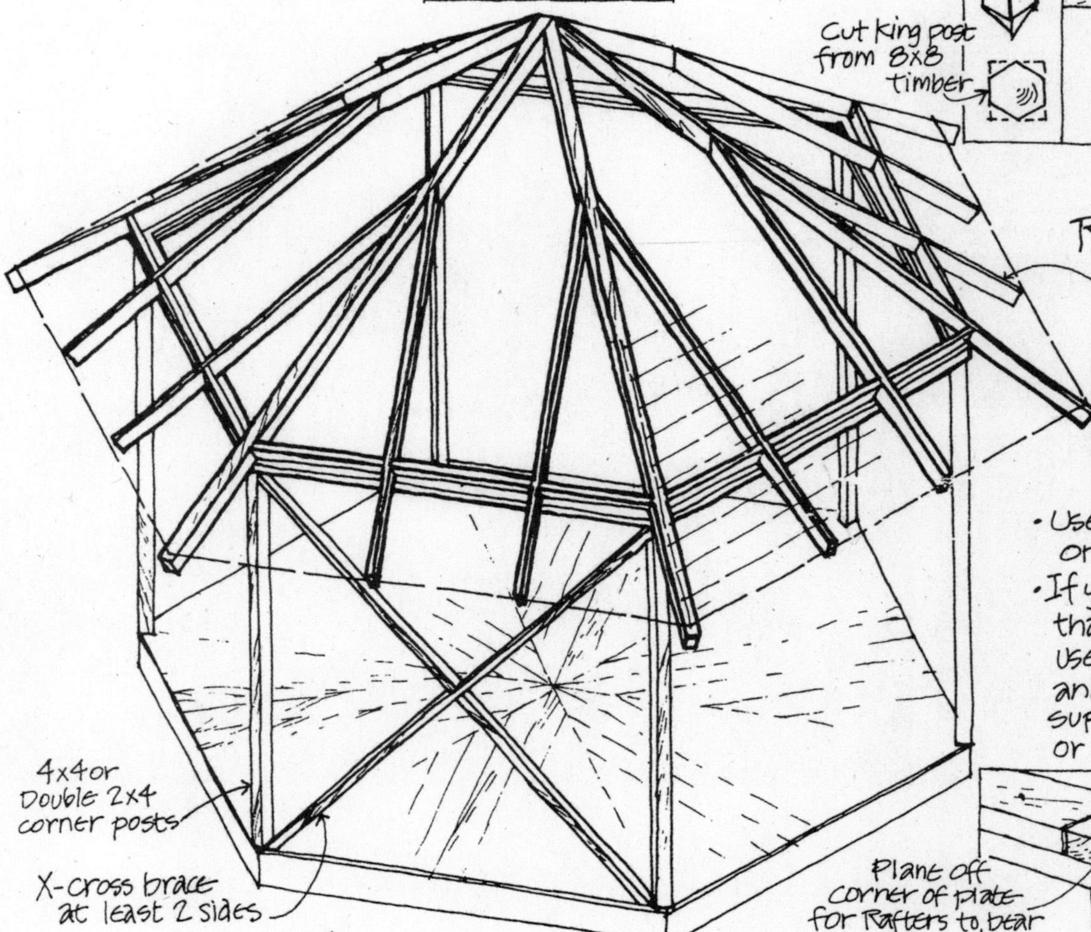

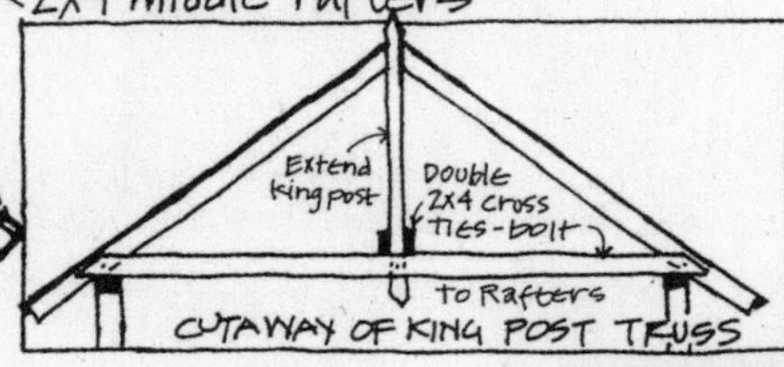

- Use 4x4 Rafters or double 2x4's.
- If you build larger than 12' diameter, use 4x6" or 4x8" Rafters, and either use center support post to floor or or king post truss.

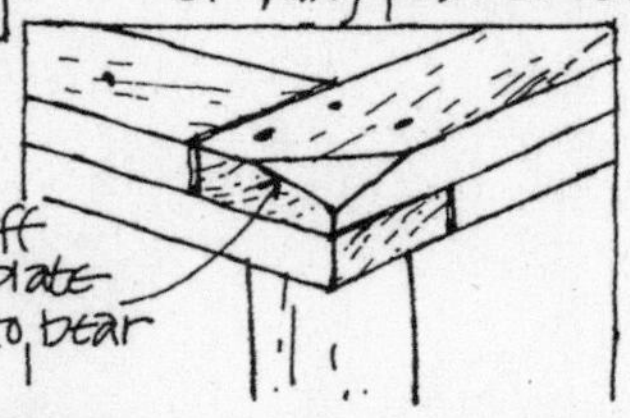

Pentagonal building at Ananda

HEXAGON 12' DIAMETER

- HEX IS EASIEST POLYGONAL BUILDING
- SEE PAGE 131 FOR MORE MANY-SIDED STRUCTURES.
- EVEN-SIDED POLYGONS EASIEST.

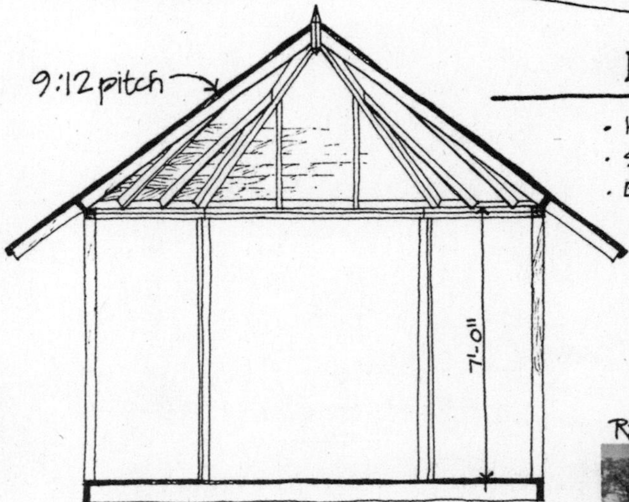

CUTAWAY THRU HEXAGON

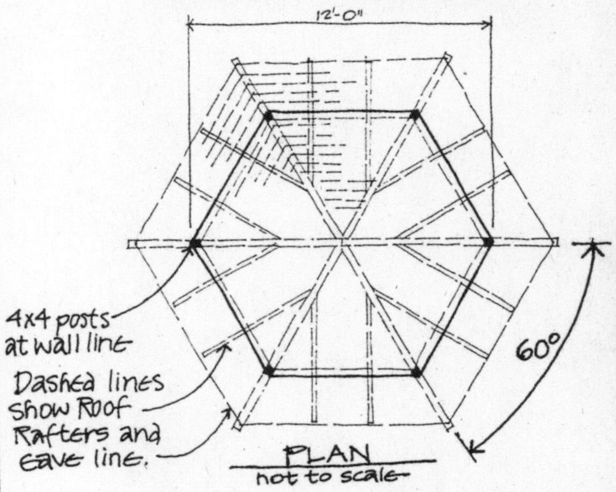

PLAN
not to scale

Random Polygon at Black Mountain, Ca.

1/2 Hex Room on house, Texas

Gazebo with carved King Post

12-sided Haberhedron built by Jack Angus

Another way to frame a small Hex roof Needs all 4x6 Lumber

Small Hex built in California by Scott Sheldon

POLYGONAL BUILDINGS...

Polygonal, or many-sided buildings, make a more interesting interior space than rectilinear buildings, but are harder to build and fit furniture into. The angle cuts you've got to make can mean that it will take you twice as long to build. Compared to geodesic domes, however, polygonal buildings are easier to build, more adaptable to used materials, easier to enlarge, and are more durable. It's also easier to put in used doors and windows in the vertical walls.

Lloyd Kahn

Bolinas, California, USA,
Since 1970s

Buildings in which we conduct our lives are mostly structures created from rectiliniar elements joined at right angles. Hexagons can appear as a way of rebelling against the tyranny of rectilinear geometry or of wanting to be seen as rebelling against the tyranny of rectilinear geometry. In some sense hexagons are organic as they occur naturally and were one of the first alternative geometries to be appropriated by architecture.

Publication: *Shelter*, p. 44

Photography: Dylan Perrenoud

Moon Ra

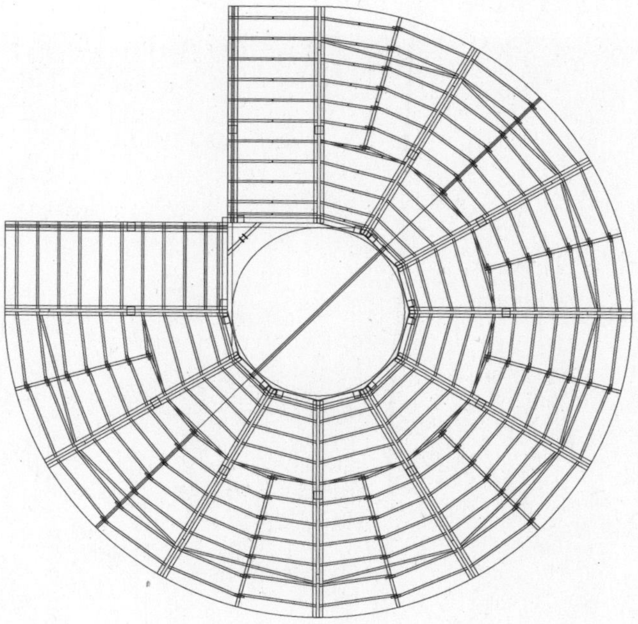

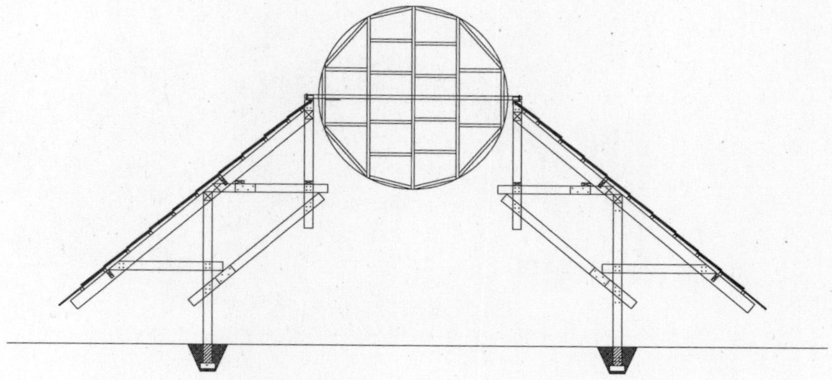

Leopold Banchini Architects

Host Festival, Brussels, Belgium, 2021 (under construction)

The project brief called for the adaption or renovation of the previous years festival stage, designed by FALA, into something new. The interest of the office, however, lay in construction rather than composition. In this vein, the previous FALA designed pavilion was not used or considered as a motif or as a formal starting point for something new. Instead the creation of the new pavilion focused on the re-use of the pavilion as an exercise in both taxonomy and reconstruction.
The tectonically recogniseable FALA pavilion, a clear composition of walls and a floor, was disassembled, catalogued and reconstructed into a hut-like roof structure punctuated by a large rotating disc above a fire pit. Festival goers were placed in direct contact with the ground and with the elements, firmly decontextualising the users from exterior happenings of the festival and of the outside world by introducing them to a more primal and intimate spatial experience.

Text: Horst Festival

Photography: Leopold Banchini Architects

60’ Red Rockers Dome

11 Men & Women

Red Rocks, Colorado, USA, 1970

Starting in the late 1960s and continuing through the 1970s, countless waves of young Americans left the cities and suburbs and moved to the country. Many joined communes such as the radical Southwest commune Red Rockers. It was one of many intentional communities like Libre or Drop City that were propagating the “access to tools” ethos of the *Whole Earth Catalog* and other do-it-yourself publications of the time. They were collectively constructing domes for an alternative way of living together. As one member of the Red Rockers put it, “we wanted to create a structure that didn’t remind us of anything—a new kind of space in which to create new selves.”

Publication: *Shelter*, p. 138

RED ROCKERS

We (about 11 men & women) built our 60 foot dome three years ago for about $2500. What we wanted was a place to all live together in order to change our lives and ourselves.

We wanted to create a structure that didn’t remind us of anything – a new kind of space in which to create new selves. We also needed a space that was large enough to house a lot of people and their trips – a space that was voluminous enough to assume different shapes as we changed and our needs changed.

The dome was the most beautiful in the very beginning – empty. From the Red Rocks (our favorite lookout point and the landmark on our land from which we took our name) it looked like a huge cut wooden gem. Then WE moved in and took over. I think there were thirteen of us the first night we slept in the dome and we were overcome with the massiveness of the space and the weird accoustics. We went immediately about the business of tacking up our pictures of Meher Baba and George Jackson. One week after we moved into the dome we had a huge Thanksgiving party (now an annual event) and there were 180 people holding hands in the pre-dinner circle.

The first winter we all slept in a circle along the wall of the dome. By the second winter we had added a kid’s room (we started having kids) and a big mezzanine style sleeping platform that extends about three quarters of the way around the dome’s circumference. The platform improved our lives a great deal because it is nice and warm there in the wintertime and most of the beds have a beautiful view through the arc of windows that serves to heat the dome on sunny winter days. Two babies have been born on the platform, one on the main floor, and last summer we delivered one in a tipi right behind the dome. We have spent a lot of time and energy getting our kitchen together. We built a big brick range with lots of gas burners and a cast iron griddle that we use every morning for pancakes, french toast and eggs from our chickens. We built counter tops and cabinets with tongue & groove oak and pine that we salvaged from an ancient ghost town dance hall nearby.

When we first put in our arc of windows we covered it with vinyl. Last spring we replaced the vinyl with plexiglass. We used fancy silicone sealant for the windows which was very expensive and totally ineffective. Last week we re-sealed the arc windows with asphalt sealant and right now we are (incredibly) without leaks. Plexiglass is o.k. but it is very expensive and scratches too easily.

In the summertime most of the Red Rockers move out of the dome into tipis or temporary shelters. This summer many of us are moving out and won’t be moving back. We plan on building four small houses this summer. These will be sleeping spaces – small shelters designed for one, two or three people, probably without kitchen facilities. After three years of living in a heap, most of us have decided that in order to keep becoming new people, to keep growing and changing, we need more privacy. We are still a communal family that wishes to hold together but we need a new kind of shelter for this period in our growth – shelters that will be places to make love in and argue in, to play music and write and worry and think and decide what the next step is to be.

The dome will continue to be a center for us. We will continue to eat together here and meet together and hang out. The platform will be converted into a sewing area, general crafts area, etc.

138

30' Wooden Dome

FLOOR FRAMING

Foundation: approx 12" diameter "Baxter Poles", the green treated poles which are supposed to last for 75 years. I think next time I'd use concrete sonotubes instead as you know they'll never rot.

Flooring: 2x8" dry tongue and groove white pine, layed in radial pattern. Bang it in with sledge hammer from the end for tight fit. To darken it I used a weed burner flame thrower (scary device), then wirebrushed. Opposite effect of stain: hard grain dark, soft wood lighter. Much work, maybe a full week in all, but beautiful. Improves with age. No varnish, sealer or wax. Just wood.

HUB

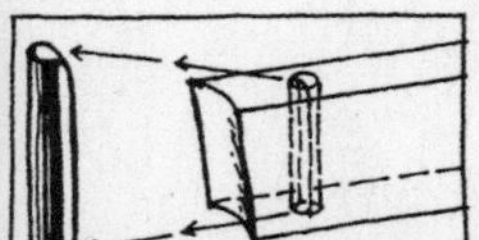

1/2 ROUND IN HOLE

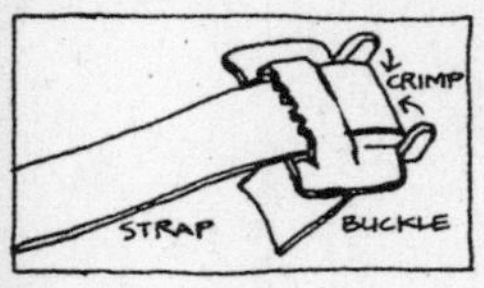

Pipe: any diameter available from Kilsby Tube Supply, San Leandro, Calif. However 2 7/8" OD water pipe is cheaper, available anywhere.

I followed the experience of Jeff Morse and used a Band-it strapper and buckles in this dome, which is stronger than the strapping we used in *Domebook 2.* Band-it Co., 4799 Dahlia St., Denver, Colo. 80216. Strapping turns out to be expensive. If I had it to do again I'd probably use the plywood hub from *Domebook 2,* maybe with wooden dowels instead of bolts – An all-wooden structure.

Strap: bought 3 rolls about 30 lbs. each, had about ½ roll left over. So used about 75 lbs. ½" .025 strap. $97.00 worth.

Buckles: about $50; *tubing:* about $95.

Struts: This assumes an understanding of the information in the Pacific Dome section of *Domebook 2* (pp. 21-22). Table is for 4-frequency alternate hemisphere, 2"x3" struts.

Strut	No. each	Chord factor	x	Radius	=	Chord length	-	Subtract hub	+	Add for rounding operation	Strut length	Axial angle
A	30	.25318	x	180"	=	45 9/16"	-	2 7/8"*	+	3/8"**	43 1/16"**	82¾°
B	30	.29524	x	"	=	53 5/32	-	3 1/8	+	"	58 13/32	81½°
C	60	.29453	x	"	=	53	-	"	+	"	58 9/32	81½°
D	90	.31287	x	"	=	56 5/16	-	"	+	"	53 9/16	81°
E	30	.32492	x	"	=	58 1/2	-	"	+	"	55 3/4	80½°
F	30	.29859	x	"	=	53 3/4	-	"	+	"	51	81½°

Essential notes on this table:

* I rounded strut ends to fit perfectly around pipe. If you don't do this; adjust accordingly.

** These lengths are based on 3 1/8" outside diameter tubing, for all but the pentagon vertexes, where I used a 2 7/8" OD tubing. I wanted 2x3 struts to pack tightly.

Windows: here is what I did with my windows:

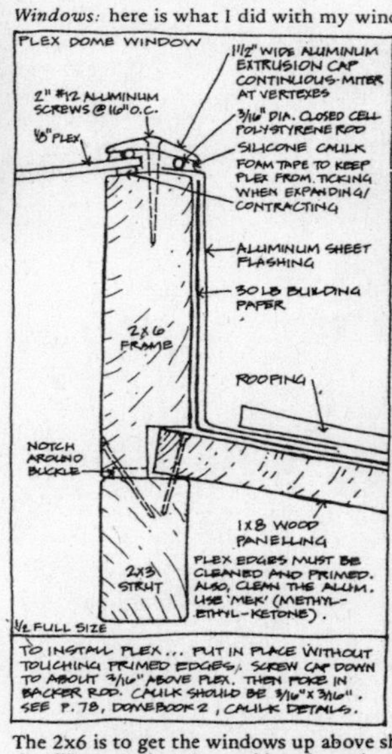

ROUNDING STRUT ENDS

The 2x6 is to get the windows up above shakes. If you use plex, the silicone sealant (everything cleaned and primed) with aluminum extrusion is the best method. However it's a very difficult, painstaking process. As careful as we were I still have a few leaks, had to get up and caulk about three times last winter.

I used 1/8" plexiglas from Swedlow, Inc. in L.A. With some other people building a dome, we bought a 51" wide roll of 2nd quality plexiglas, about 2400 lbs., cost about 35 cents per sq. ft. I got some aluminum extrusions from Jeff Morse and followed his window details (¾ *Dome* in *Domebook 2*) with a few changes: I used a backer rod for spacing, and put some foam tape between the plex and wood so it wouldn't tick during expansion-contraction.

A friend who manufactures skylights loaned us his large machine shop for a night and we were able to use a carbide tipped blade especially designed for plexiglas to cut all our window pieces. Without the use of this shop we would have had much trouble handling and cutting this much plastic.

Plexiglas is the best plastic window material, but you must be meticulous in measuring, cutting, cleaning and caulking. Its disadvantages compared to glass is it scratches easily, collects dust and probably will turn yellow in ten years. Working with it you must keep in mind that it expands and contracts tremendously with temperature changes. Thus give it room, never put two pieces of plex next to each other, or to another material where it will bind when expanding: if you must bolt through it, use oversized holes. Jeff Morse discovered that you can use silicone sealant for a hinge.

WOODEN DOME

Even after some years disillusionment building various domes I tried one more. This one was an attempt to blend the dome concept and wood construction. A final dome experiment. In some ways it worked, but in most it didn't. A description of the construction follows, because if someone is intent on having a dome, the framework and window details here are better than anything in *Domebook 2.* However, because this dome photographs well I'd like to point out its drawbacks before giving construction details. If you're thinking of building a dome home, I hope you'll think about the following things I've learned the hard way:

1. Building a dome, you are locked into abstract math, the computer that worked out measurements and angles. The frame is relatively quick and light, but the rest is hard. Putting in doors, windows, the kitchen, trying to fit 90° furniture against changing-angled walls: time consuming, frustrating. You can't innovate, improvise as with perpendicular walls. The polyhedron you've started with is pure form, unyielding to changes.

2. In the midst of cutting up 10' 2x3's for struts, 14-16' 1x8's for panelling I realized these short pieces would not be salvageable, unless for another dome. Wood can be used over and over, but each time it's shortened you diminish choices of the next builder.

3. I used shakes for the exterior because I found redwood logs on a beach and split them. However, although they look good, it was difficult and wasteful: shakes are made for flat surfaces, fitting them on a building with over 100 triangular planes and changing angles is maddening and difficult. Then, as you get up around the top of the dome you must cut shakes into pie shapes to fit the tightening circle: wasteful. In addition the slope at the top is too shallow for shakes to keep wind or water out.

4. I couldn't use salvaged doors and windows for entry and light, had to buy new plexiglas. Now I want more doors opening out, but just don't have the energy to fight the shell and weaken it in framing them in.

5. What generally excites people at first about a dome is the openness, the purity, yet this is precisely what stops me from making subdivisions, which would look awkward. Thus I ended up with a one-room house in which all sounds, smells and vibes are on top of everyone. O.K. for one person, or someone not needing privacy. After 4 years living in domes, the excitement of moonlight through overhead windows has worn off. Now we'd rather step out to look at the skies, and often yearn for a low-ceilinged wooden room, fireplace with bed nearby.

6. I'm afraid the dome won't last long, because the entire building is roof, it gets full weather treatment over entire surface, unlike a building with vertical walls and roof acting as umbrella for rain and sun. Domes require more maintenance and have a much shorter life span than rectilinear buildings.

Is it all bad? No, although it has many difficulties as a home, it makes a wonderful space for working in, a studio (or a large space to be spanned, such as an auditorium or theater). In fact, we're putting together this book in the dome, so it does have its functions. However, if you are considering building a dome, I urge you to read through the 32 pages of dome building information in this book.

136

Lloyd Kahn

Bolinas, California, USA, 1970s

Lloyd Kahn's publications on dome-building from the early 1970s were filled with notes, plans, and observations, along with letters, photos, and insights from dome-builders around the country. His *Domebook 1* was a modest success, but it was his 1971's *Domebook 2* that became the biggest seller and a catalyst for what would become a nationwide dome boom. The geodesic dome built by himself that is depicted here was even featured in *Life Magazine* at the time. After 5 years of dome building and dome living however, Kahn concluded that "domes didn't work as homes, and were in fact, a poorer and less practical way of enclosing space as compared to rectilinear construction." As a result he took *Domebook 2* out of print.

Publication: *Shelter*, p.136

Atelier Hawkesbury

Leopold Banchini

Hawkesbury river, New South Wales, Australia, 2021

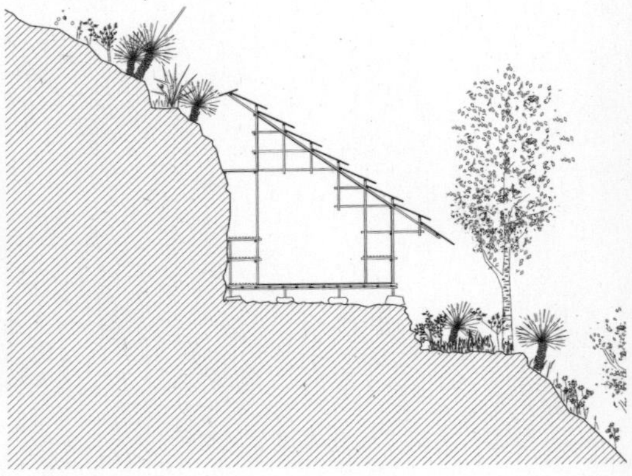

In the early 1990s, Richard Leplastrier settled on the shore of Lovett Bay, the mouth of the Hawkesbury river. Describing the wonderful house, he wrote: “The house continues a history of simple living on the site, which I suspect has continued for thousands of years [...] Our family of five lives comfortably in this one room. The small room we inhabit, in turn, inhabits a greater room whose walls are cliffs and floors the tidal level of the bay that rises and fall nearly two meters every six hours.”
Atelier Hawkesbury is another small room built along the same river. Accessible by water only, the projects uses a minimum amount of resources and takes advantage of the existing land. Leaning against the sandstone rocks, the lightweight structure is entirely made of 1×1" local wood joists and studs. The large staggered roof protects from the heavy rains while allowing the light to filter through. Translucent polycarbonate sheets enclose the brightly lit volume while preserving a constant dialogue with the surrounding forest and changing light. The stone cliff who protected the Wannungine and the and the Darkinyung people for countless years invites itself inside the house and becomes simultaneously wall and landscape.

8' × 12' Shed

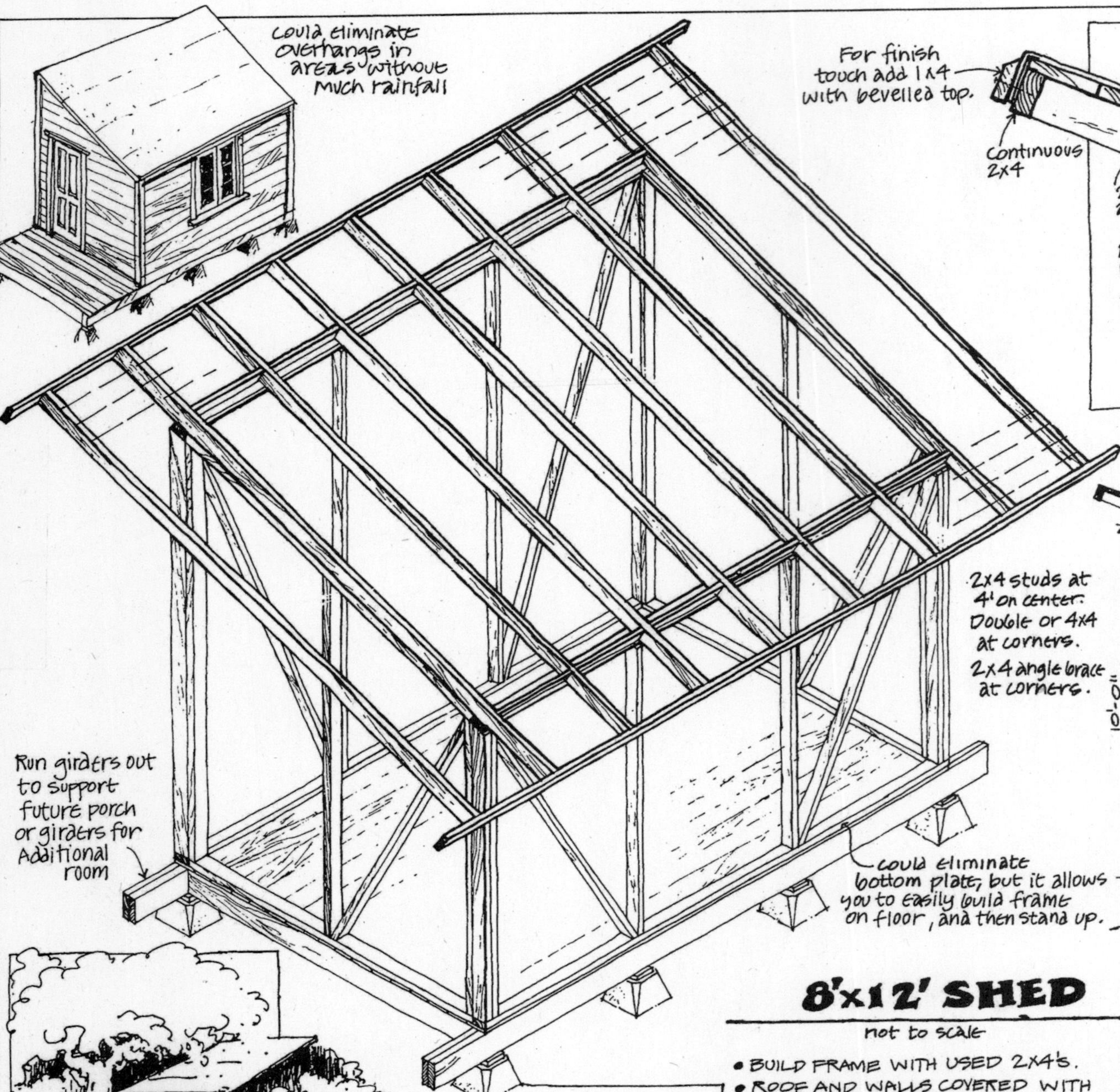

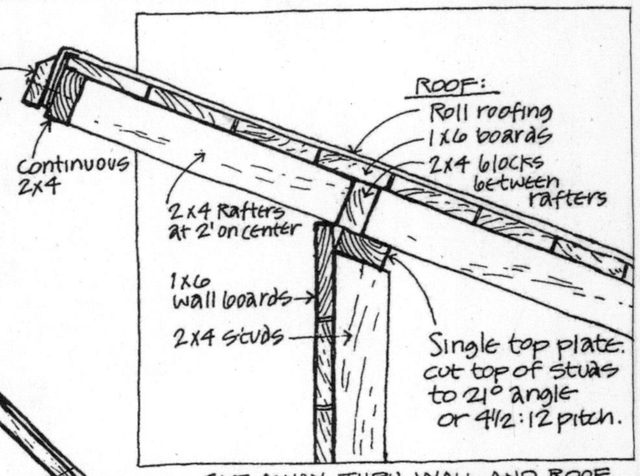

CUT AWAY THRU WALL AND ROOF

All studs and rafters nailed with 2-16d common nails. Used wood is very hard, use american made nails.

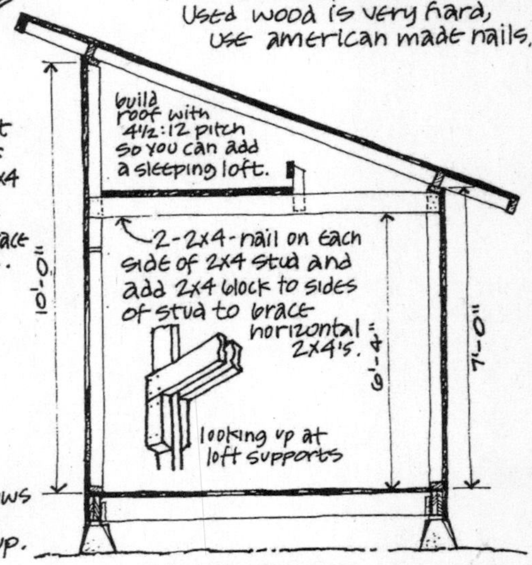

CUT AWAY THRU SHED

8'x12' SHED

not to scale

- BUILD FRAME WITH USED 2x4's.
- ROOF AND WALLS COVERED WITH SALVAGED 1x6 BOARDS.
- SEE PAGE 58 FOR FLOOR FRAMING, PAGES 60-62 FOR WALLS, WINDOWS, DOORS, ROOFING.

Will Wood built his shed house next to a huge rock with part of the roof raised for a loft.

Loft in shed under raised roof. Built by Kelly Hart.

add another room to shed

porch added to shed

Kelly's shed, center left. Will Wood's workshop.

Siting...

If you plan to build a dwelling, before you decide on a design or materials, you should consider the site: how you will be affected by sun, wind, rain, summer and winter climate, roads, outlook, trees, neighbors, cars, birds...Ideas about structure will appear to you from these considerations. It would be ideal to camp out on your site for a year and watch the changes before building anything.

An alternative would be to build a small shed to the side of your site and live there for a year before deciding what to do next. You could watch the angle of the sun change throughout the year, learn where the winter storms come from, and figure how to have the morning sun at your breakfast table. You could see how to catch cool breezes in the summer and see the stars at night. Also, you'd have time to meet the neighbors, study their houses, talk to the old folks about elements peculiar to the area: special winds, drainage problems, sources of cheap materials: local wisdom about local problems.

Point is: don't approach your site with preconceived notions. The site, and what surrounds it, should have the strongest influence on whatever is placed upon it. In the ancient Chinese art of *feng-shui*, "...building location and design is based on a belief that at every place there are special topographical features, either natural or artificial, which indicate or modify the cosmic energies present there. The forms and arrangements of hills, the nature and directions of watercourses, the heights and forms of buildings, the locations of forests, roads and bridges are all important factors. The influence of the sun, the moon, the planets and the stars are also considered important...."

Feng-Shui, Ernest J. Eitel, Hong Kong, 1873.

Some siting tips:

- If your buildable area is limited, first determine what and where your waste disposal (septic system or outhouse, compost pile) must be located.
- Sun angle: in most areas, a roof overhang can let in low winter sun, and block the hot (and higher) summer sun. Skylights that face south and/or west will let in a lot of summer heat.
- Winds: you can site your building to block the prevailing winds so you can have a protected outdoor area. Winds follow the canyons, in hot areas, there is usually a breeze in ravines. Storms batter buildings built on hilltops, exposed sites.
- Study old buildings that are still in good shape in your area, check their siting and materials.

Build your shed to the side of where you would imagine your main room. Later, you could easily attach a larger building to a simple shed, or leave it separate as a guest room or shop. This shed, and the buildings shown on the next pages are simple prototypes for new builders to start from, and are designed to be built from used and salvaged wood. On page 50 are listed other books that have practical building information.

Lloyd Kahn

Bolinas, California, USA,
Since 1970s

A shed is a simple shape to build, sheds water and snow better than a flat roof, and is a good shape for later additions or extensions. It is also a good shape for adding to an existing building. Clerestory (high) windows are often installed on the high side of a shed roof building, allowing high light to enter without the waterproofing problems of skylights.

Publication: *Shelter*, p. 40

Photography: Dylan Perrenoud

Casa CCFF

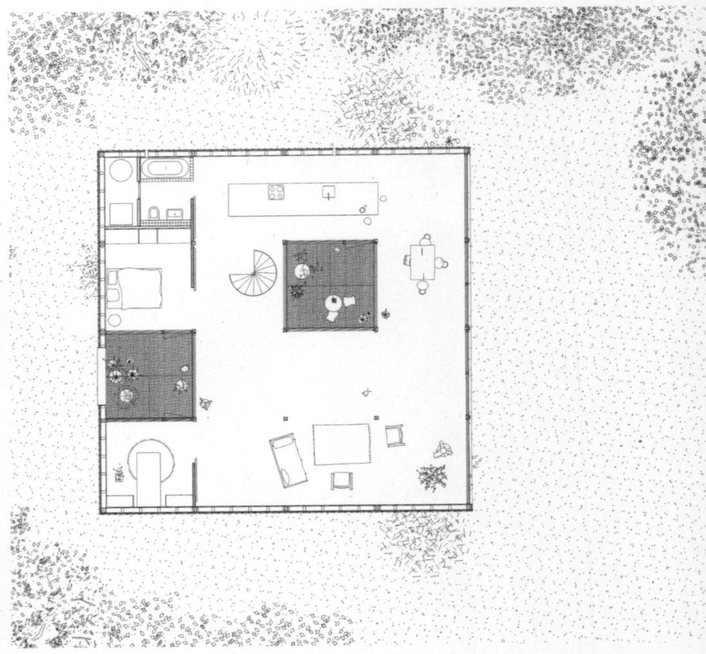

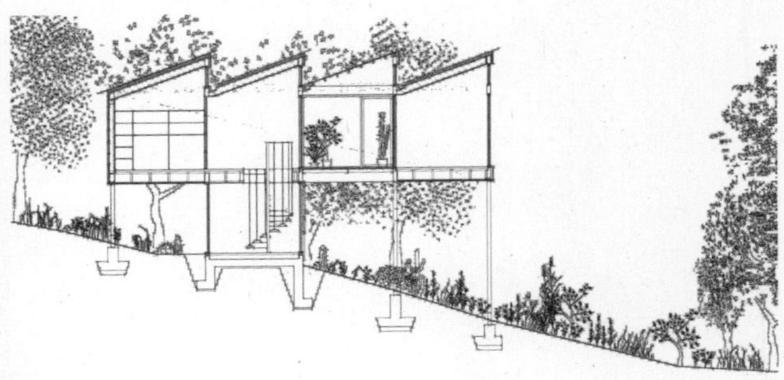

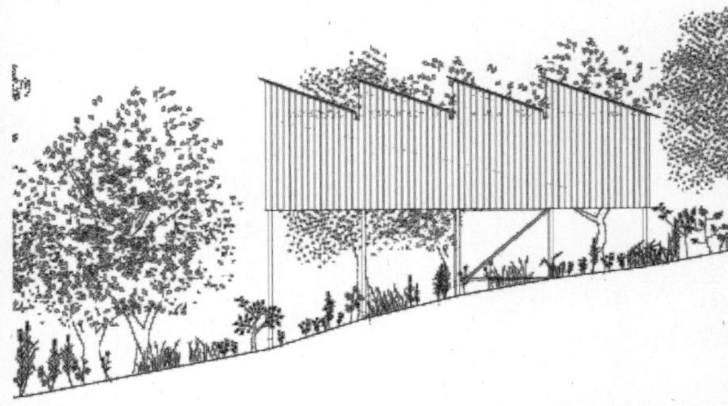

Leopold Banchini Architects

Geneva, Switzerland, 2018

Casa CCFF is a domestic factory floating above an untouched garden. Mimicking the surrounding industrial shed roofs, the large open volume is filled with sunlight. The views to the exterior are carefully framed to create a brightly lit intimacy in this highly urban environment.
On the first floor, two interior gardens divide the living spaces and bring nature to the heart of the house. Overlaying transparencies blur the boundaries between interior and exterior. Under the suspended volume, a generous covered space allows for outdoor living and parking. Each architectural element placed in the square plan is specifically designed for the simple house. Casa CCFF is an eco-friendly urban house overlooking Geneva's industrial train station. Using economical materials and prefabrication, it reduces the construction costs to the minimum. Developed with engineer Marc Walgenwitz, the house is built almost entirely in wood, pushing the structural capacities of this natural material to its limits and reducing the use of concrete to a bare minimum. Achieving high insulation values and maximising solar gain, a small heat pump allows to avoid the use of fossil fuels. Assembled in a few days by local carpenters, the small house proposes an alternative to the archetype of swiss concrete houses often lying on heavy foundations.

Photography: Dylan Perrenoud

14' × 20' Hip

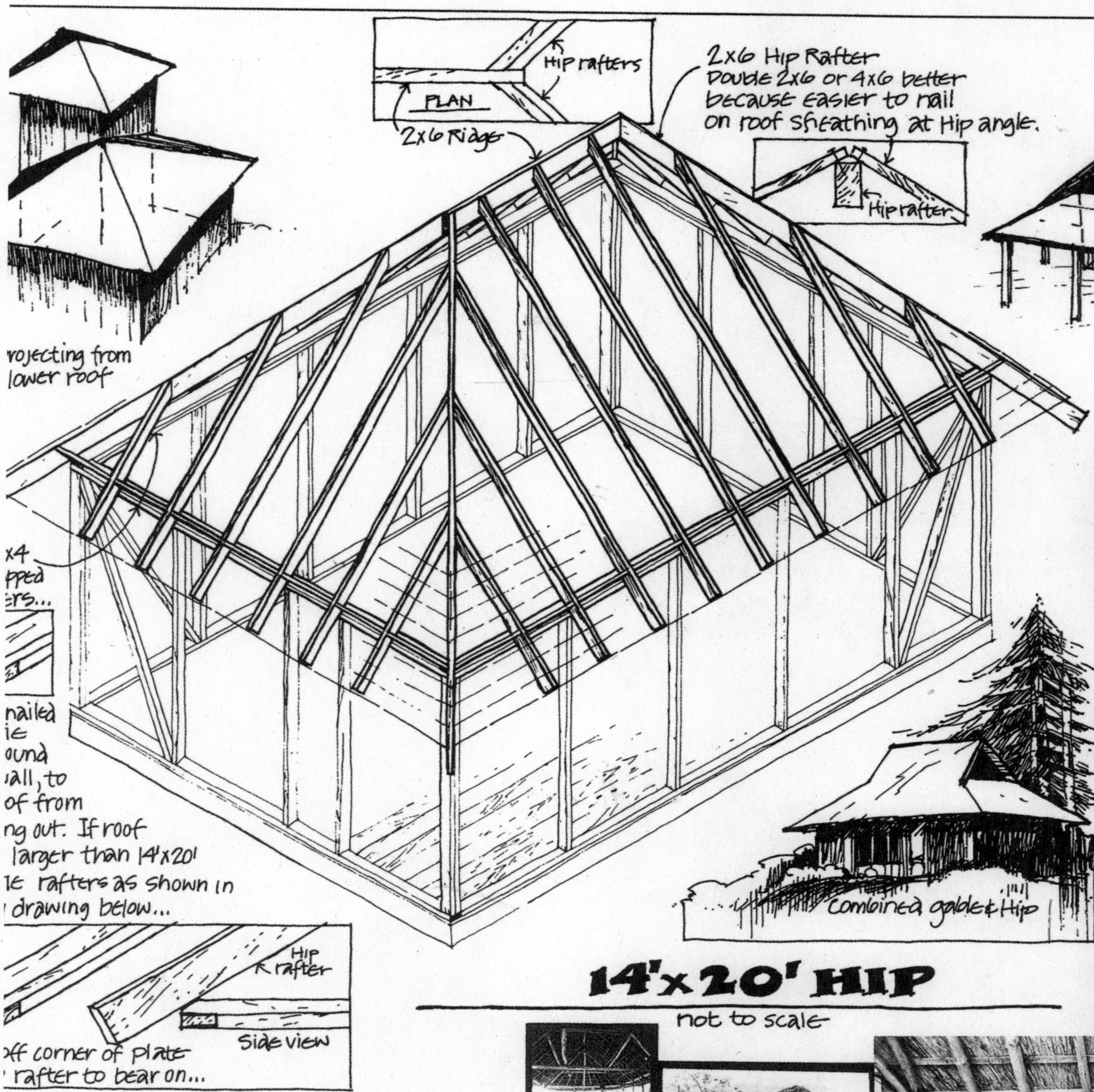

Hipped tower built by Robbie Robinson

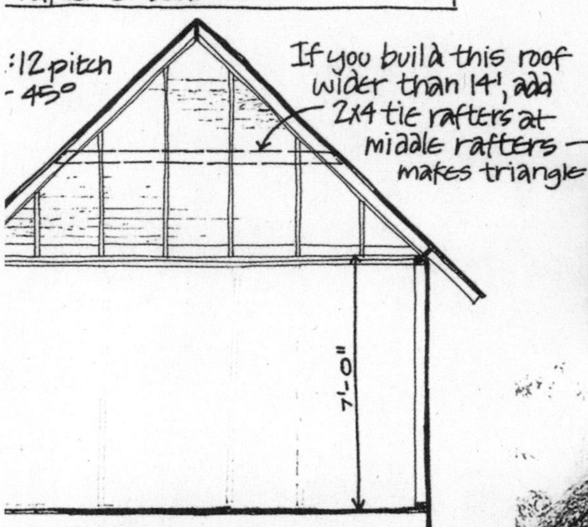

CUTAWAY OF HIP ROOF

roof is built by many people around the ainly in areas of heavy rainfall. It seems to er protection from the weather than a gable rotects all four sides of the building with its line. It's the most common framing system hing in tropical areas, built with poles and pe, but whatever the roofing material, the shape is beautiful from the inside and outside.

Yucatan

Lloyd Kahn, Robbie Robinson

Bolinas, California, USA,
Since 1970s

A hip roof is a type of roof where all sides slope downwards to the walls. Thus, a hipped roof house has no gables or other vertical sides to the roof. Hip roofs are more difficult to construct than a gabled roof, requiring more complex systems of rafters or trusses. Hip roofs can be constructed on a wide variety of plan shapes. Each ridge is central over the rectangle of the building below it. In modern domestic architecture, hip roofs are commonly seen in bungalows and cottages, and have been integral to styles such as the American Foursquare.

Publication: *Shelter*, p. 42

Photography: Dylan Perrenoud

Villa Marramarra

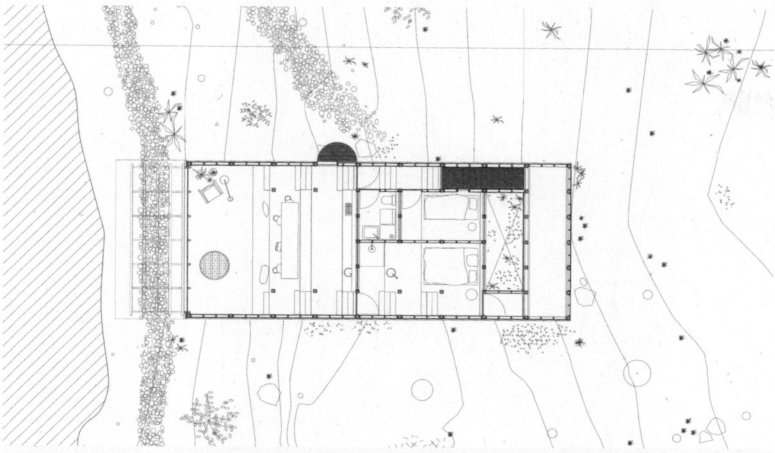

Leopold Banchini Architects

Marramarra Creek, Berowra, Australia, 2020

Villa Marramarra is an off-grid timber dwelling located on the banks of Marramarra Creek, a tributary of the Hawkesbury River only accessible by boat.
The stepped longitudinal section in conjunction with a tightly arranged structural grid simply and clearly acknowledge the steeply sloping site upon which the house is located. Spatially the interior of the house is entirely focused on one large north-facing window orientated towards the creek edge. The window is split in half and can be hoisted upwards allowing the densely wooded, chaotic site into the tranquil timber lined interior space of the house.
The house is constructed entirely of cheaply available stick lumber and the footings are pinned to the underlying sandstone bedrock, avoiding the need for heavy concrete footings and reducing the impact on the site as well as the number of trades required during the construction process to a bare minimum. Both solar energy and water are collected on the roof and stored on site.

Text : Tobias Beale

Photography: Leopold Banchini Architects

24' × 32' Gambrel

A gambrel roof is a usually symmetrical two-sided roof with two slopes on each side. The usual architectural term in eighteenth-century England and North America was "Dutch roof." The upper slope is positioned at a shallow angle, while the lower slope is steep. This design provides the advantages of a sloped roof while maximizing headroom inside the building's upper level and shortening what would otherwise be a tall roof.

Publication: *Shelter II*, p. 98

Gambrel

Gambrel roofs are most often found in the eastern part of the United States and Canada. The word derives from the hock (bent part) of a horse's leg, also called a gambrel. The lower part of the roof is a steep slope, the upper part shallower. The break in roof line allows head room in the loft space, and is useful in barns for hay storage (see pages 102-103 for gambrel barn plans), as well as in homes for rooms above plate level.

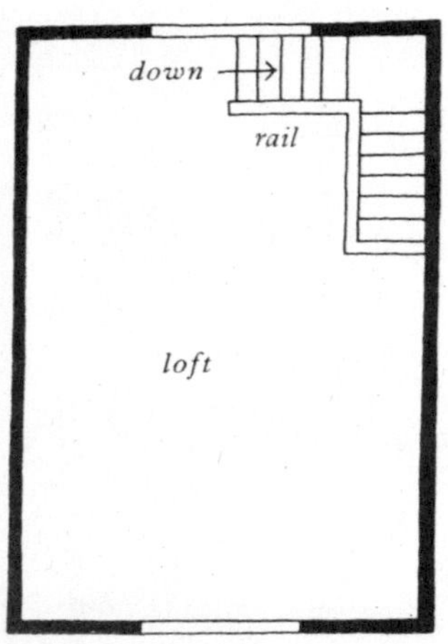

Loft plan

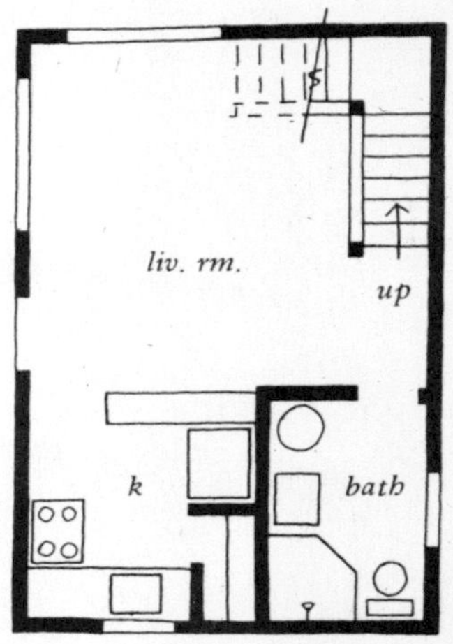

Main floor plan
scale: 3/32" = 1'-0"

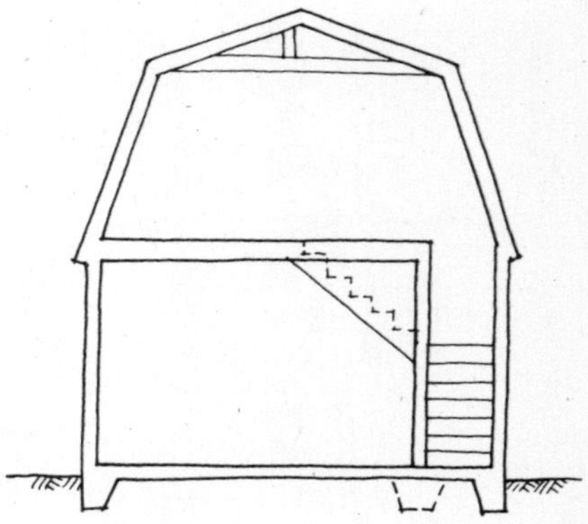

Cross section

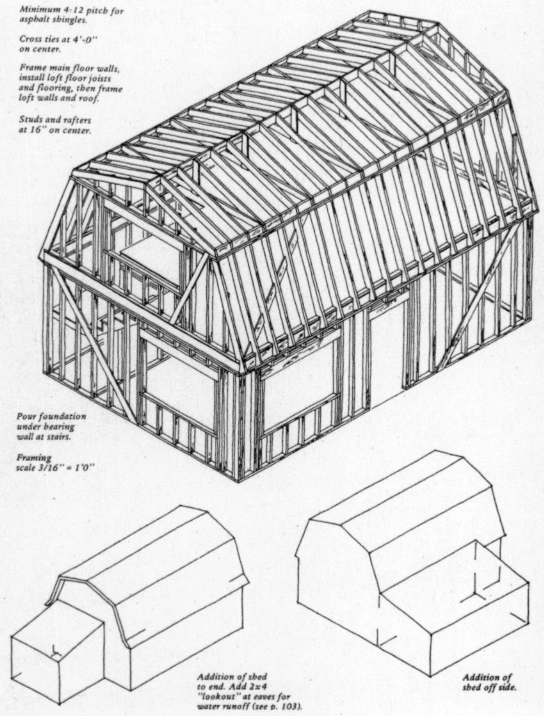

The Magic Is Still There

Leopold Banchini, Lukas Feireiss, Lloyd Kahn, Dylan Perrenoud

In January 2020 architect Leopold Banchini and curator Lukas Feireiss together with photographer Dylan Perrenoud travel all the way from Europe to Bolinas, an unincorporated coastal community approximately an hour northwest of San Francisco. Known for its reclusive residents and unmarked roads, this community has been home for more than half a century to 85 year old publisher and builder Lloyd Kahn and his wife Lesley Creed. Founding editor-in-chief of *Shelter Publications*, and former Shelter editor of the *Whole Earth Catalog*, Kahn is also an author, photographer, and pioneer of the building and green architecture movements. After a first tour around their half-acre homestead, a conversation sparks in Lloyd's densely filled production studio and office. A simple building, made from torn-down Navy barracks at Treasure Island on San Francisco Bay in the 1970s.

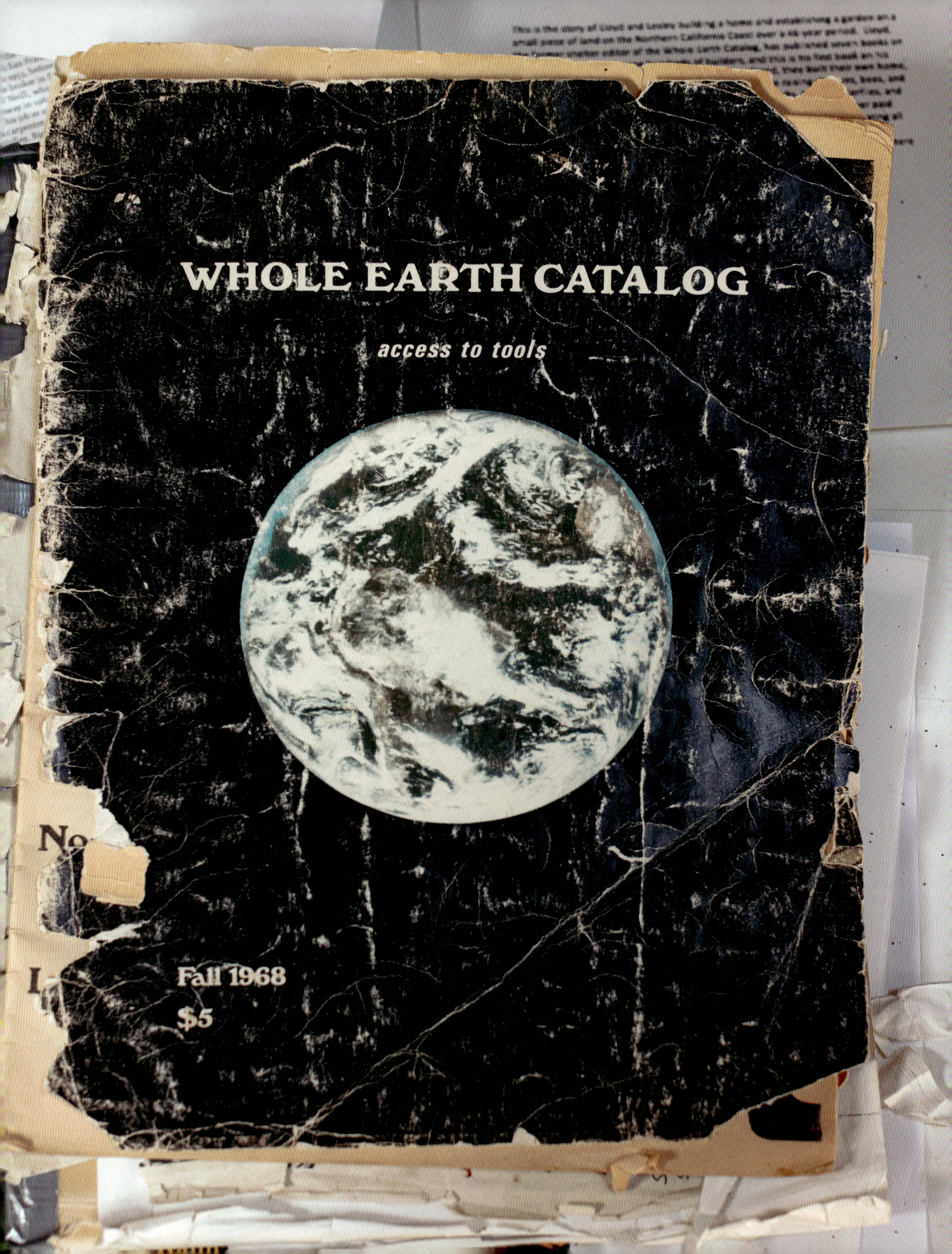
WHOLE EARTH CATALOG
access to tools
Fall 1968
$5

LLOYD KAHN
So what is this all about?

LUKAS FEIREISS
That's a very good question. Let's start by contextualizing everything. The upcoming Architecture Biennial in Venice curated by Hashim Sarkis is asking: *How will we live together?*[1] Originally Leopold was invited to show the permanent installation *3–8*, he made for the Centre Pompidou in Paris in the exhibition section in the Arsenale dedicated to the topic of Households. However instead of showing an already existing work, Leopold proposed to speculate upon the content of three iconic counterculture publications on organic architecture published half a century ago by you—namely *Domebook One* (1970), *Domebook 2* (1971) but most importantly *Shelter* (1973). At this point Leopold reached out to me to collaborate on this project. I work as a curator of exhibitions and editor of books in the field of art, architecture, design and contemporary cultural reflexivity, and we've known each other because the two of us were running Master of Fine Art and Design programs at the Sandberg Instituut in Amsterdam for a couple of years. So this is how it all came about. Now our contribution to the Biennale is in many ways an homage to you and your work as publisher and builder from an architectural as well as curatorial point of view. And despite all formal differences, I actually sense a similar fascination and appreciation of simple everyday building materials in both of your work.

LK
So you are building houses, Leopold?

LEOPOLD BANCHINI
Yes. I tend to build houses everywhere I live. Currently I live in Geneva, Switzerland where I also grew up. Even though I actually sold the house that I originally built for myself there (see page 36). Before that I was living in Lisbon, Portugal but my wife is Australian. So right now we are building a little house off the grid there. Only accessible by boat. Very nice place not far from Sydney (see page 32).

LK
How far by boat?

LB
It's only 15 minutes from the Marina, which is accessible by train from Sydney center.

LK
So you hire a boat to take you out there?

LB
I have a tiny boat, one of this aluminium flat one.

LK
How many meters long?

LB
It's three and a half meter. Tiny.

LK
Like my boat here, twelve foot. How much horsepower?

LB
20.

LK
Yeah.

LB
It's quite an amazing place. But that aside, I work in the middle East as well. I am doing a project in Bahrain at the moment that incorporates the traditional construction method of using palm tree leaves which are tied by rope to build walls (see page 21).

LK
I've got lots of books on all kinds of different natural materials that would interest you. I didn't realize that you were into that. Some really good books on bamboo, that are kind of rare. But anyway.

LB
Yes, coming back to the Biennale, one of the things that I find fascinating in your books are the various de-growth models that can be discussed again as serious alternatives to conventional forms of building today almost half a century later. They raise serious questions of ecological awareness as much as they inquire the very notion of what makes up a household. All of these questions are still highly relevant for me today. So I wonder if we haven't really learned so much in the last fifty years?

LK
Well, one of the things that happened when I finished my new book, *The Half-Acre Homestead*, I looked at it and I thought, this is what we talked about doing in *Shelter* 49 years ago.[2] And at the beginning of *Shelter*, we said to go back to things that were discarded for a long time, like actually doing things with our hands again. Some of these traditions from the past are worth taking another look at now, for example, in building your own house. With my new book I basically followed what we laid out in *Shelter*: Do it yourself. Use your hands.

Back then in 1960s and 1970s it was in many ways a golden era in America because you could live on very little money and try out a lot of things. Lesley and I for example had an income of $300 a month for the two of us back then and we got by. We all wanted to go out and get 10 acres in the country and build a log cabin and live independent and be self-sufficient. It's different nowadays. You don't need to go as far. You do what you can. Maybe find a little house in a city, in a rundown neighborhood, to buy and fix up; or find a loft in the city and convert it into a living space or simply grow some chives and some parsley on your fire escape. You don't have to do everything. Self-sufficiency is a direction. You never attain it. I realized that when I tried growing wheat. There are all these processes that you need to go through in planting and harvesting wheat until you get to flour, that it just doesn't make sense to do it on your own. It's better to buy that from somebody else.

LF
Your book *Shelter* has sold over 300,000 copies until this day, which speaking as a book maker myself, is an absolutely astonishing number. So there still seems to be quite some interest in alternative building methods.

LK
Yes. A thing that's been happening in the last few years is that I have a lot of young people in their 20s and 30s discovering *Shelter* and telling me that this is what they want to do. It's a totally different generation. That's hopeful to me. The message remains the same: Do what you can for yourself with your hands. They are also asking me how they can actually do it. When I was building in the early 1960s, I was an insurance broker during the day and then I would come home and work every night and on the weekends. But if you can save enough money to live on for a year, buy your groceries and pay your bills, you can build a house in that year. Putting away enough money is maybe gonna take you five years or ten years but it's possible. I also think that the act of physically building things is a great balance and antidote to our digital world.

LF
What do you think makes *Shelter* such an inspiring book?

LK
It's the people in *Shelter* that are so inspiring. Their personal stories. Their ways of living. I had a guy come up me to some years ago at a green festival. Real big guy. He told me, "I remember when I first saw this book. It was at a party. I ended up sitting in some corner and reading the book all night. I quit my job the next morning and I started building. Now I'm a contractor." Hearing stories like this is the real payoff to me. I think Shelter motivated thousands and thousands of people to do something. It connects.

LF
You were saying that you originally worked as an insurance broker before. So how did it all start for you?

LK
Well, from 1958 to 1960, I was in the Air Force, running a newspaper on a base in Germany. When I got out of the Air Force, I came back home and we bought a piece of land in Mill Valley from where I commuted to San Francisco. I was in business with my father, my uncle and my brother. At that same time there were so many creative things happening in San Francisco. Poetry, music, the

1
As curator of 17th International Architecture Exhibition—La Biennale di Venezia 2021, the Lebanese educator, architect and Dean of the School of Architecture and Planning at the Massachusetts Institute of Technology aims to capture the structural problems and ongoing changes of contemporary society around the world. He says: "In the context of widening political divides and growing economic inequalities, we call on architects to imagine spaces in which we can generously live together: together as human beings who, despite our increasing individuality, yearn to connect with one another and with other species across digital and real space; together as new households looking for more diverse and dignified spaces for inhabitation; together as emerging communities that demand equity, inclusion and spatial identity; together across political borders to imagine new geographies of association; and together as a planet facing crises that require global action for us to continue living at all. The participants of the Biennale are encouraged to engage other professions and constituencies—artists, builders, and craftspeople, but also politicians, journalists, social scientists, and everyday citizens."

2
In 1974, Lloyd Kahn and his wife Lesley Creed started building a home and establishing a garden on a half-acre piece of land on the northern California coast. The book tells their story with over 500 photos of their home, the garden, pantry, kitchen, green-houses, chicken coop, and animal visitors.

Beatniks.[3] So on my lunch hour I would sometimes walk up to Upper Grant Avenue. There was a place called the Co-Existence Bagel Shop.[4] They had poetry readings and jazz there. That's where I read *Howl* by Allen Ginsberg for the first time.[5] So I was basically a straight guy who was looking over at all this other stuff going on. Then probably in 1964, I started smoking pot. That really got me into the other side of my brain. So a year later in 1965 I took a leave of absence for one month and I hitchhiked across the country. Went to New York, went out to Cape Cod to visit my cousin who was a painter, living in Provincetown. Hitchhiking back into New York city. I got picked up by these three guys who are going to the Rhode Island School of Design and on their way to a Bob Dylan concert that night.[6] So I came along. It was three dollars to get in. I said that I was a journalist so I was right up next to the stage with my camera. It was maybe his second or third concert where he switched from folk music to rock and roll. Anyway, I got home and i quit the insurance businesses and went to work as a carpenter in Big Sur. First year I worked on a big house made from huge bridge timbers. I was the foreman, I've made four dollars an hour. And the guys I went with, two brothers, they got three dollars an hour, and we lived on a ranch, in a chicken coop, while we were building this house. After that I built my own house.

LF
Was this around the time that you got interested in dome buildings?

LK
Yes, I got really interested in building domes. I ended up spending two years at Pacific High School, which was a hippie high school in the Santa Cruz mountains, where we built 17 geodesic domes out of all kinds of different materials. Out of that came *Domebook One* and then *Domebook Two*. A couple of years later I moved out here. At that point I still hadn't given up on domes so I built a really nice looking dome here. But then I concluded that they didn't work out. I took the dome down and *Domebook Two* out of print, even though it was selling well. When I called my agent, he thought I was crazy, but I just didn't want any more domes on my karma. Admitting you're wrong in front of a couple of hundred thousand people is not something that you really want to do. But I did. I said, look, I made a mistake and I am sorry about that. It just doesn't make any sense to do a building from an abstract concept like an icosahedron or polyhedra. It's not worthwhile as a basis for construction.

LF
So was *Shelter* basically your way of making things right again?

LK
With *Shelter* we said, here's what it's really all about. People and buildings from all over the world. Africa, Hong Kong, Canada and the United States. Here's what they're doing. This is what really got me into doing books on building, even though I didn't do any books for three or four years after *Shelter*. I was going to be a farmer but we eventually found out that we couldn't make a living being farmers. Back then people wouldn't pay for organic food. So then I did *Shelter II*, which isn't really like the first book at all. It's actually a very good book on building a stud frame house.
I built domes for five years before I discovered the simplicity of rectangles. I remember driving out to a resort on a lake in the Santa Barbara mountains to do the layout for *Domebook Two*, with an IBM Electric Composer typesetting machine and Polaroid MP-5 camera on an easel I borrowed from *Whole Earth Catalog*.[7] I was looking at the buildings on the side of the road—chicken coops and barns—fascinated by their simplicity. Just a vertical wall and a roof that's just one plane. Not all these different angles. So I eventually became a convert to that type of construction. At least for where I live. If i lived in the desert, that would be adobe.

LF
It takes courage to learn from your mistakes.

LK
If you're wrong, just say you're wrong. Once you admit you're wrong, it's okay. My life is a series of mistakes. I said, look, this is what I thought back then but I don't think that anymore. I've contemplated the idea and I've come to a new conclusion. You shouldn't be afraid to try something new, because you'll learn from it. This goes on to this day with me.

LF
Since you just mentioned Stewart Brand's *Whole Earth Catalog* for which you served as Shelter editor, it made me think of an expression by Brand in the same line of thought the so called a "fiasco-by-fiasco-approach to perfection."[8] So how did you meet in the first place anyway?

LK
I met Stewart when I was still building geodesic domes. We were into the same things, he was just much further along getting all of this information together. The first *Whole Earth Catalog* he put out in 1968. It was 5 Dollars, 64 pages, printed on a newspaper press and it combined many of the things everybody was interested in in the 1960s. This counterculture publication sold over 3 million copies.

LF
So what were your inspirations and influences at the time?

LK
Buckminster Fuller was a real inspiration for me and my friends, although I later came to find out that he didn't even invent the geodesic dome.[9] The first geodesic dome was designed by the chief engineer of the Carl Zeiss optical company in Jena in 1926 in Jena, Germany.[10] Fuller just didn't give credit to the people. He didn't invent the Tensegrity sphere either.[11] That was done by a student of his. Fuller's ideas were also just wrong. A big, clear, sphere over New York City? Bad idea. The Dymaxion car was not only a rip off of an early Fiat model, but it was dangerous too. It killed somebody. So anyways, in the beginning, he was a great influence. Other than that, Zen Buddhism. Shunryu Suzuki Roshi, a beautiful man.[12] I started already when I was an insurance broker. Going to meditation at five thirty in the morning in San Francisco. Also architects like Bernard Maybeck[13] and Frank Lloyd Wright,[14] although later I had some reservations about him too.

LF
Despite your later criticism of Buckminster Fuller, it must be said that he was at least intent on finding solutions to the great problems of mankind—like the housing problem.

LK
I think solving mankind's housing problem was a bad idea. In particular if you're trying to do it with geodesic domes, instead of understanding the building site and where the wind comes from and what the weather is like for example. Most architects are not interested in doing what's simple. They are interested in making a statement. Sometimes you can learn more by looking at a farm building.

LB
Yet, it seems as if there was still a sense of utopia in 1960s and 1970s—a belief in the possibility of radical change—that has been lost today.

3
The term Beatnik was a media stereotype prevalent throughout the late 1940s, 1950s to mid-1960s that displayed the more superficial aspects of the Beat Generation literary movement. Over time the name ended up being applied indiscriminately to both the stereotype, and artists of the Beat Generation and its followers. The Beat Generation was started by a group of authors whose work explored and influenced American culture and politics in the post-war era. The central elements of Beat culture are the rejection of standard narrative values, making a spiritual quest, the exploration of American and Eastern religions, the rejection of economic materialism, explicit portrayals of the human condition, experimentation with psychedelic drugs, and sexual liberation and exploration.

4
The Co-Existence Bagel Shop was a Jewish deli in North Beach, San Francisco that became the home of the Beat movement. American writer and pioneer of the Beat Generation Jack Kerouac (1922–1969) mentions the Bagel Shop in his semi-autobiographical novel *Desolation Angels* published in 1965.

5
Allen Ginsberg (1926–1997), American poet, philosopher, and writer. Together with William S. Burroughs and Jack Kerouac, he formed the core of the Beat Generation. Ginsberg is best known for his poem "Howl" in which he denounced what he saw as the destructive forces of capitalism and conformity in the United States. San Francisco police and US Customs seized "Howl" in 1956, and it attracted widespread publicity in 1957 when it became the subject of an obscenity trial, as it described heterosexual and homosexual sex at a time when sodomy laws made homosexual acts a crime in every state.

6
Bob Dylan (*1941), American singer-songwriter, author, and visual artist. Much of his most celebrated work dates from the 1960s, when songs such as "Blowin' in the Wind" (1963) and "The Times They Are a-Changin" (1964) became anthems for the civil rights movement and anti-war movement. His lyrics during this period incorporated a wide range of political, social, philosophical, and literary influences, defied pop-music conventions and appealed to the burgeoning counterculture.

7
The *Whole Earth Catalog* (WEC) was an American counterculture magazine and product catalog published several times a year between 1968 and 1972, and occasionally thereafter, until 1998. The magazine featured essays and articles, but was primarily focused on product reviews. The editorial focus was on self-sufficiency, ecology, alternative education, do-it-yourself, and holism, and featured the slogan "access to tools."

8
Stewart Brand (*1938), American writer and visionary, best known as editor of the *Whole Earth Catalog*. He founded a number of organizations, including The WELL, the Global Business Network, and the Long Now Foundation.

9
Richard Buckminster Fuller (1895–1983), American architect, system theorist, author, designer, inventor, and futurist. Fuller published more than 30 books and developed numerous inventions, mainly architectural designs, and popularized the widely known geodesic dome.

10
The Zeiss Planetarium in Jena, Germany has been in operation for more than 90 years, making it the oldest continuously operating projection planetarium in the world. Its opening in 1926 was revolutionary in many respects—for the natural sciences and technology, cultural theory and media history—and not in the least for its architecture. The Jena planetarium was a completely new building type. Its thin-walled dome, which Zeiss engineer Walther Bauersfeld developed together with structural engineer Franz Dischinger, represented a milestone in the history of building construction.

11
The tensegrity sphere or so called *Cloud Nine* is the name Buckminster Fuller gave to the proposed airborne habitats created from giant geodesic spheres, which might be made to levitate by slightly heating the air inside above the ambient temperature.

12
Shunryu Suzuki (1904–1971), Zen monk and teacher. Suzuki helped popularize Zen Buddhism in the United States and is renowned for founding the first Buddhist monastery outside Asia. He founded San Francisco Zen Center which, along with its affiliate temples, comprises one of the most influential Zen organizations in the United States. A book of his teachings, *Zen Mind, Beginner's Mind* (1970), is one of the most popular books on Zen and Buddhism in the West.

13
Bernard Ralph Maybeck (1862–1957), American architect in the Arts and Crafts Movement of the early 20th century. He was an instructor at University of California, Berkeley. Most of his major buildings were in the San Francisco Bay Area.

14
Frank Lloyd Wright (1867–1959), American architect, interior designer, writer, and educator. He designed more than 1000 structures, of which 532 were completed. Wright believed in designing structures that were in harmony with humanity and its environment, a philosophy he called organic architecture.

PURE GARDEN FRESH
DARJEELING TEA
PRODUCE OF INDIA
2018
Sunshine

A HANDY HINT FROM
HOME OR
WORK.
GET THE
FOR THE
JOB!

LK

Well, there is no utopia. But yes, we did think the world was going to change and it did actually if you think about it. In many ways the 1960s transformed the world. Computers really came from Stewart Brand. Steve Job's described the *Whole Earth Catalog* as the Google of its time.[15] Or think of organic farming, organic food, ecological awareness, political activism and so forth. Obviously there was also a naiveté with me as well as other people hoping that's its going to be a better world, in which we're going to treat each other and our planet well. But for what went wrong, all you have to do is look at Trump. How did we ever get this loathsome creep? In the last two or three years the people in power are reversing all the ecological safeguards. But you go on, nothing is completely one way or the other. The 1960s were a wonderful time for some years. Learning all these different things from ecology to blues, and from communicating with dolphins to Zen. None of it was new but they were discovered by a large population group—the baby boomers—who had the time to pursue these alternative pathways. That was a big change.

LF

San Francisco was at the heart of this movement wasn't it?

LK

Yes, in January 1967 there was this big gathering in a large meadow in Golden Gate Park here in San Francisco, called The Human Be-In, and 10,000 people or more showed up.[16] The Grateful Dead[17] and Jefferson Airplane[18] played on trucks. They had speakers like Timothy Leary,[19] Alan Ginsberg, Gary Snyder[20] and Suzuki Roshi. It was one of these sweet spots in time when everything comes together. So the day was right and the vibes were good. At the end of that day, Ginsburg asked everyone over the microphone to practice some kitchen yoga and pick up after themselves. We left the park totally clean. That was an event everybody was inspired by and the news spread across the country. Then in June of 1967 the Monterey Pop Festival was another such magical event.[21] So these two festivals were picked up on by the whole nation and everybody came to San Francisco. 100,000 kids and San Francisco wasn't ready for it at all. No place for them to stay, no sanitary facilities, no food. That's when things went south. Drugs also came into the picture. So what they call the summer of love was actually a kind of nightmare. I am actually writing a book about this because I don't agree with hardly any of the books written about what really happened in the 1960s.

LB

Interesting. So another thing I find very intriguing about your books at this time, such as *Shelter* but also the dome books, is that they proposed models of entirely different typologies for living together.

LK

Living together? Do you mean like communes?

LB

Yes, for example. I grew up in some sort of commune in Switzerland myself. My parents generation was still very inspired. Do you have any experience with that?

LK

Communes basically didn't work. Maybe the commune where you lived was successfull. Today only a few of them are still around but for most of them it simply didn't work. In particular those that were based on anarchy and drugs. I lived on a commune once for two years but I didn't want anything to do with the commune. I wanted to get my own piece of land. I didn't want to have to make decisions with other people, so I don't know about living together if that's really going to happen.

LB

Apart from actually living together in communes, your books nonetheless offer examples of a different way of thinking about what makes a home and what a household consists of. To me the 1960s are a period in which classical notions of domestic typologies were radically questioned. One of the reasons, I believe, domes are still fascinating is because their shape simply forces you to rethink how to spatially organize yourself within a household.

LK

Well, one good thing about domes was that building them was a great collective experience of working together with others. Inspired by our dome books, a group called the Red Rockers, built a 60 foot dome out in Colorado and they all lived in the dome as well. After a year or two however, they started building little houses outside the dome to live in. You just can't subdivide a dome or add onto it.

LB

It's not necessarily about living together maybe, but your dome books, and most importantly *Shelter* really open up a new horizon on how to think with an open mind about the concept of living *per se*.

LK

Sure. The trouble nowadays is that you can't experiment like we did 40 years ago anymore because everything is so much more expensive and you need to make a living. What motivated me however with *Shelter* was never questions of typologies as such but simply construction by hand: Different methods of construction, different materials that I saw and believed to be really great. I simply wanted to show them to people. That's my motivation really for all of my building books.

LF

In that way you are also very much a storyteller. Earlier you mentioned that *Shelter* is filled with personal narratives of people talking about their buildings. I think it's never good arguments or hard facts that stick with people but good stories.

LK

I've been a communicator since I was a little kid and I will always want to tell people about what I see. Too much so, really. I have done 7,000 blog posts but it doesn't make any money. Not to mention all this work on Instagram. Now I have to get back and focus on books to keep us afloat. The new book is a story too. It's the story of our life here.

LB

So let's talk about the story of this house that you've been living in for more than forty years with your wife Lesley.

LK

In a certain sense it's a rather conventional story in that it's a man and a woman. We've had two kids that grew up here and a kitchen. A nuclear family as they call it.

LB

Yet, there's something very organic in the construction of this place. You feel that it was not designed in one go by an architect.

LK

Yeah, that's true. I built this house over time but what I realized after I had finished the book is that the book is really about Lesley. It's all her. I mean the way it looks, the food, the ambiance, the garden. She's the captain of the ship. She runs this place. When I travel, she stays here. She doesn't want to go anywhere and she does all these incredible things. I mean her quilts are simply amazing. So the house feels good to people that walk in here. The colors are warm, all the little paintings on the wall and the fact that the kitchen is a working kitchen. The Feng Shui is good. I think that's a very important part of everything.

LF

So what makes a good home in your opinion?

LK

Well, people that get along for one thing. I mean, Lesley and I, we've never had a fight. My first marriage for 15 years was disastrous in that regard. She had a difficult time with her former boyfriend too. So we both ended up separated and found each other and said "Oh you like to get along? You don't like to fight?" I guess the other elements were for us to have a roof over our heads, a garden and a place to cook, eat, sleep, heal and have friends around. That's

15
The late Steve Jobs, former CEO of Apple Computer and Pixar Animation Studios referred in his commencement address at Stanford University in 2005, to Brand's *Whole Earth Catalog* as "Google, in paperback form" in terms of importance, and referenced its mantra of "Stay Hungry, Stay Foolish."

16
The Human Be-In, event in San Francisco's Golden Gate Park Polo Fields on January 14, 1967. It was a prelude to San Francisco's Summer of Love, which made the Haight-Ashburgy district a symbol of American counterculture. The Human Be-In focused the key ideas of the 1960s counterculture: personal empowerment, cultural and political decentralization, communal living, ecological awareness, higher consciousness (with the aid of psychedelic drugs), acceptance of illicit psychedelics use, and radical liberal political consciousness.

17
The Grateful Dead, American rock band formed in 1965 in Palo Alto, California. The band is known for its eclectic style, which fused elements of rock, folk, country, jazz, bluegrass, blues, gospel and psychedelic rock; for live performances of lengthy instrumental jams; and for its devoted fan base, knows as "Deadheads."

18
Jefferson Airplane, American rock band based in San Francisco, California. One of the pioneering bands of psychedelic rock. Formed in 1965, the group defined the San Francisco Sound and was the first from the Bay Area to achieve international commercial success.

19
Timothy Francis Leary (1920 – 1996), American psychologist and writer known for his strong advocacy of psychedelic drugs. Leary believed that LSD showed potential for therapeutic use in psychiatry. He used LSD himself and developed a philosophy of mind expansion and personal truth through LSD. During the 1960s and 1970s, he was arrested numerous times worldwide. US President Richard Nixon once described Leary as "the most dangerous man in America".

20
Gary Snyder (*1930), American man of letters. Perhaps best known as a poet (often associated with the Beat Generation and the San Francisco Renaissance), he is also an essayist, lecturer, and environmental activist with anarchoprimitivist leanings. He has been described as the "poet laureate of Deep Ecology." Snyder is a winner of a Purlitzer Prize for Poetry and the American Book Award. His work, in his various roles, reflects an immersion in both Buddhist spirituality and nature.

21
The Monterey International Pop Music Festival, three-day concert event held June 16 to June 18, 1967 at the Monterey County Fairgrounds in Monterey, California.The festival embodied the theme of California as a focal point for the counterculture and generally is regarded as one of the beginnings of the "Summer of Love" in 1967.

NO PARKING PLEASE

where you start from and then you go off and do what you're going to do in life. A good home to me is also something that's continually changing. We're changing things this week for a fact. It's constantly evolving. It's an accumulation of tasks that probably produce a pretty good result when you're doing it yourself as opposed to slam bang building construction.

LF
I suppose it's been a huge learning process too.

LK
One of the things I learned through building was that if you start, you'll figure it out.

LF
A very basic rule of life.

LK
Indeed. It's just like I say to people, if you're timid or you don't know what to do, just start. That can really be anything in life. If you start, you will figure it out. The momentum of it all will cause you to learn as you go along. When I'm working on a book for example, I just do two pages at a time. Other people have a have whole outline set up and organized before they even start with the first page. I also say to young people who don't know how to build their house themselves to hire a carpenter and work with him and learn from him, or hire a plumber and work with him and so forth. I won't have time to do it in this life, but I wish I could start over again building this house, because of what I've learned up to now. So all these things that I would do, they're very different from what I ended up with.

LF
That's life, ain't it? As German philosopher Immanuel Kant said
"Out of the crooked timber of humanity, no straight thing was ever made."[22]

LK
Yeah. Imperfect. The good thing about thinking like that is that I can tell other people for example: Look, if I started now I would have a central core with a woodstove with a hot water coil in it, so you heat your water in the wintertime with the fire. And on the roof I would have a solar panel that would heat the water in the summertime. I would basically try to get part of a house built with plans to add on later. Get a roof up first to be able to live and cook in it while finishing of the rest of the house. If I say that to people they maybe take my advice and can do some of those things better than i did.

LB
I have a totally different question for you, Lloyd. I have noticed that you dedicated a whole section to mushrooms in your new book. We're actually also planning to work with mushrooms for the installation at the Venice Biennial. With fungus predating humans by over a billion years and predicted to survive the next climate catastrophe, and against the backdrop of contemporary reassessment of the mushroom, advancements in mycelium as a sustainable material and as a metaphor for our entangled existence, the fungi here serve as a symbolic element to us that offers the promise to reimagine our current relationship with the planet.

LK
Well, it's funny because we just spoke about mushrooms last night. One of my best friends is a botanist and a mushroom expert. He can look at any mushroom and give you the Latin name for it. We've been talking about a new book called *Underland: A Deep Time Journey* Robert Macfarlane, who, amongst other things, talks about the underground networks of roots and by which trees and mycelium communicate.[23] So if a tree over here, is attacked by a beetle, it basically sends a message through the roots to this tree over there saying "watch it, this beetle is coming to you. Develop some antibodies to fend off this beetle".

LF
The so called Wood Wide Web.[24]

LK
It's just this amazing underground world that's been going on forever that we didn't know about. So yeah, mushrooms are really fun. I've been collecting mushrooms for about ten years now and I do it whenever I can. I used to go running once a week on the beach with my friends but now we walk because we're too old. We were all competitive runners and but now we meet every Tuesday at six o'clock. So last night and I had three baskets of mushrooms with me in order to find out their names and which ones can and can not be eaten.

LF
Flipping through your new book *The Half-Acre Homestead* right now, I was wondering if you could just read out that little paragraph you wrote about all the different ideas, concepts, perceptions, movements and discoveries that were going on in the 1960s? It's very powerful.

LK
Sure. You mean this one? Zen Buddhism, meditation, the Tarot, the Kabbalah, the I Ching, martial arts, women's liberation, gay rights, the sexual revolution, Black Power, Native American culture, marijuana and LSD, political activism, building your own house, organic gardening and farming, revival of crafts, alternative energy, store energy sources, sun wind and water, ecological awareness, self-sufficiency, the Beat poets, blues and rock and roll, the Beatles, Rolling Stones and Bob Dylan, *Rolling Stone* magazine, dozens of other new underground newspapers, dolphin consciousness, viewing the Earth from space, the *Whole Earth Catalog*, planetary consciousness, whole systems, the West Coast publishing revolution, the first desktop computers, domes, long hair, new styles of dressing, the human being and the Monterey Pop Festival ... I could do a podcast with this. Everybody's been encouraging me to do podcasts.

LF
You should. Definitely.

LK
By the way, there's two books I really recommend. One is called *Sex at Dawn*[25] and the other is called *Civilized to Death*;[26] both are by Christopher Ryan. Really good books. He does podcasts too. There's all these different ways to communicate for somebody like me. There's books. Okay, and then there's pamphlets and posters and then there's Instagram, twitter and writing a blog. Facebook, I just can't deal with. Then I've rediscovered Email recently. Email is almost old school these days. It's different from social media, because the stuff I put out on social media goes out to everyone around the world. But with email it goes directly to you. Did I send you guys the Give me Shelter newsletter?

LB
Yes.

LK
Okay. So that's another means of communication. I'm trying to figure out now which of these things to use to communicate and at the same time make a living. I'm kind of walking a tightrope here trying to get enough money from books to finance our operation going on here which is much more than just books. I mean we're answering questions about all kinds of things. Shelter Publications is really a hub of communication. So it's an exciting time now. Podcasts are another means of communication that I haven't really explored yet but all these young people are telling me to do. When I just read that paragraph to you it gave me the idea to make that into a podcast. So excuse for thinking out loud here and jumping all over the place. When are you guys going to Venice?

LB
The Biennial starts towards the end of May and runs all year long.

LK
I've never been to Venice. I hear it has a lot of problems right now.

LB
True. It has a lot of problems, but still remains a quite a special place, I have to say.

LK
Yeah, that's just like San Francisco and New York. You can complain about it, but the magic is still there.

22
Immanuel Kant (1724–1804), Prussian German philosopher in the Age of Enlightenment. The quote derives from his 1784 essay entitled "Idea for a Universal History with a Cosmopolitan Purpose."

23
Underland: A Deep Time Journey by British writer Robert Macfarlane, published in 2019. Underland is a book about the deep-time pasts and futures of the Earth, as revealed by mythical underworlds and real subterranean journeys.

24
Current research has shown that beneath every forest and wood there is a complex underground web of roots, fungi and bacteria helping to connect trees and plants to one another. This subterranean social network, nearly 500 million years old, has become known as the "wood wide web."

25
Sex at Dawn: The Prehistoric Origins of Modern Sexuality, 2010 book about the evolution of monogamy in humans and human matting systems by Christopher Ryan and Cacilda Jethá. In opposition to what the authors see as the "standard narrative" of human sexual evolution, they contend that having multiple sexual partners was common and accepted in the environment of evolutionary adaptedness.

26
Civilized to Death: The Price of Progress, 2019 book by Christopher Ryan that explores the ways in which "progress" has perverted the way we live: how we eat, learn, feel, mate, parent, communicate, work, and die. It counters the idea that progress is inherently good, arguing that the "progress" defining our age is analogous to an advancing disease. In Civilized to Death, Ryan makes the claim that we should start looking backwards to find our way into a better future.

THE COMPACT EDITION OF THE OXFORD ENGLISH DICTIONARY
VOLUME I A-O
VOLUME II P-Z
OXFORD
SHELTER
TINY HOMES
庇护所
ホームワーク
TINY HOMES ON THE MOVE
Shelter II
THE ELEMENTS OF TYPOGRAPHIC STYLE
MONGOLIAN Cloud Houses
WILDWOOD WISDOM
Shelter, Shacks
FEED ME
TWININGS

UNSEAL
ADHESIVE
RELEASING
SOLVENT
LOCTITE
Kerosene
Odorless, 1-K Grade
Paint
Thinner
DIABLO
SCREEN AND SPLINE INSTALLATION TOOL
stud THUD
Valvoline
KROIL

United States of America Hydrological Map
Waterways based on Strahler Stream Order

All That the Rain Promises and More...
ARORA
ALL THAT THE RAIN PROMISES, AND MORE ...
A Pocket Field Guide to Mushrooms
by DAVID ARORA
David Arora
Mushrooms Demystified
SIEGEL SCHWARZ
MUSHROOMS of the Redwood Coast
MUSHROOMS

Catalog of Mycological Curiosities

Lukas Feireiss, Mariangela Beccoi

This Catalog of Mycological Curiosities pays homage to the fascinating world of fungi—one of the oldest and the largest living being, which is neither an animal nor a plant and predates humans by over a billion years. As a metaphor for our entangled existence, the fungi thereby serves as a symbolic element that offers the promise to reimagine our current relationship with the planet. The following pages follow a similar organizational approach in the interweaving of topics and ideas as Lloyd Kahn's publications, and pays tribute to his fascination with mushrooms. Reading this is like searching for mushrooms in the woods. This section is thereby at once a copy, a combination, and a creation.

Alice's Adventures in Wonderland

Illustration of Alice talking with the Caterpillar for the first edition of *Alice's Adventures in Wonderland*, 1865

Alice's Adventures in Wonderland written by Charles Lutwidge Dodgson under the pseudonym Lewis Carroll, is one of the most popular works of English-language fiction. Since its first publication in 1865, the novel has never been out of print and it has been translated into at least 97 languages.
"One side will make you grow taller, and the other side will make you grow shorter." One side of what? The other side of what?" thought Alice to herself. "Of the mushroom" said the Caterpillar, just as if she had asked it aloud; and in another moment it was out of sight. Alice remained looking thoughtfully at the mushroom for a minute, trying to make out which were the two sides of it; and as it was perfectly round, she found this a very difficult question. However, at last she stretched her arms round it as far as they would go, and broke off a bit of the edge with each hand".
Author: John Tenniel;
Source: Wikimedia Commons

Amanita muscaria

Amanita muscaria, commonly known as fly agaric in reference to the medieval practice of breaking the caps into a saucer of milk in order to stupefy flies (Albertus Magnus, *De Vegetabilibus*, 1256), is probably the most iconic and widely recognazible toadstool species featured worldwide in many aspects of popular culture. The red and white-flacked mushroom, though it is generally considered poisonous, is famed for its psychoactive and hallucinogenic properties noted since 4,000 years ago to indigenous people of Siberia and Sami Indians that used it as an entheogen.
Author: Vera Kratochvil;
Source: Public domain pictures

Photo of a specimen of Amanita muscaria

Armillaria solidipes

The blue whale has been considered for long time the largest living organism on Earth for its ability to grow approximately 33 metres in length and weight 200 tons. However the discovery in 1998 of an Armillaria solidipes (previously called Armillaria ostoyae) of at least 9,6 square kilometres expansive growth—an area equivalent to 1665 football fields—in Oregon's Malheur National Forest, forced scientists to revise their idea of the largest as well as the oldest living organism on Earth, with a growth estimated to be between 1,900 and 8,650 years old.
Author: Henk Monster;
Source: Wikimedia Commons

Photo of a specimen of Armillaria solidipesniger

Amanita caesarea

Amanita cesarea is a widespread and highly regarded edible ectomycorrhizal mushroom native to southern Europe and North Africa. While it was first described by Italian mycologist Giovanni Antonio Scopoli in 1772 as Agaricus caesareus, its common name Caesar's mushroom comes from being a favourite of the Roman emperors the Caesars.
It is said that Agrippina sleekly used it to plan the death of her husband emperor Claudius. By preparing Amanita caesarea, his favourite dish, laced with the juice of Amanita phalloides, the toxic fungus known as the death cap, she ensured the rise of her son Nero to emperor of Rome in A.D. 54.
Author: Lazaregagnidze;
Source: Wikimedia Commons

Photo of a specimen of Amanita caesarea

Arpanet

The Advanced Research Projects Agency Network (ARPANET) is considered the precursor of the internet. It was developed under the direction of the US Advanced Research Projects Agency in 1967, with the initial purpose to communicate with and share computer resources among mainly scientific users. Soon ARPANET met the needs of military command and was operated by the US Defence Department during the two decades of its existence, until 1990.
American mychologist Paul Stamets coined the term "Earth's Natural Internet" based on the strong similarities he observed in the 1970s between the mycelia underground networks and ARPANET.
Credit: The Computer History Museum;
Source: Wikimedia Commons

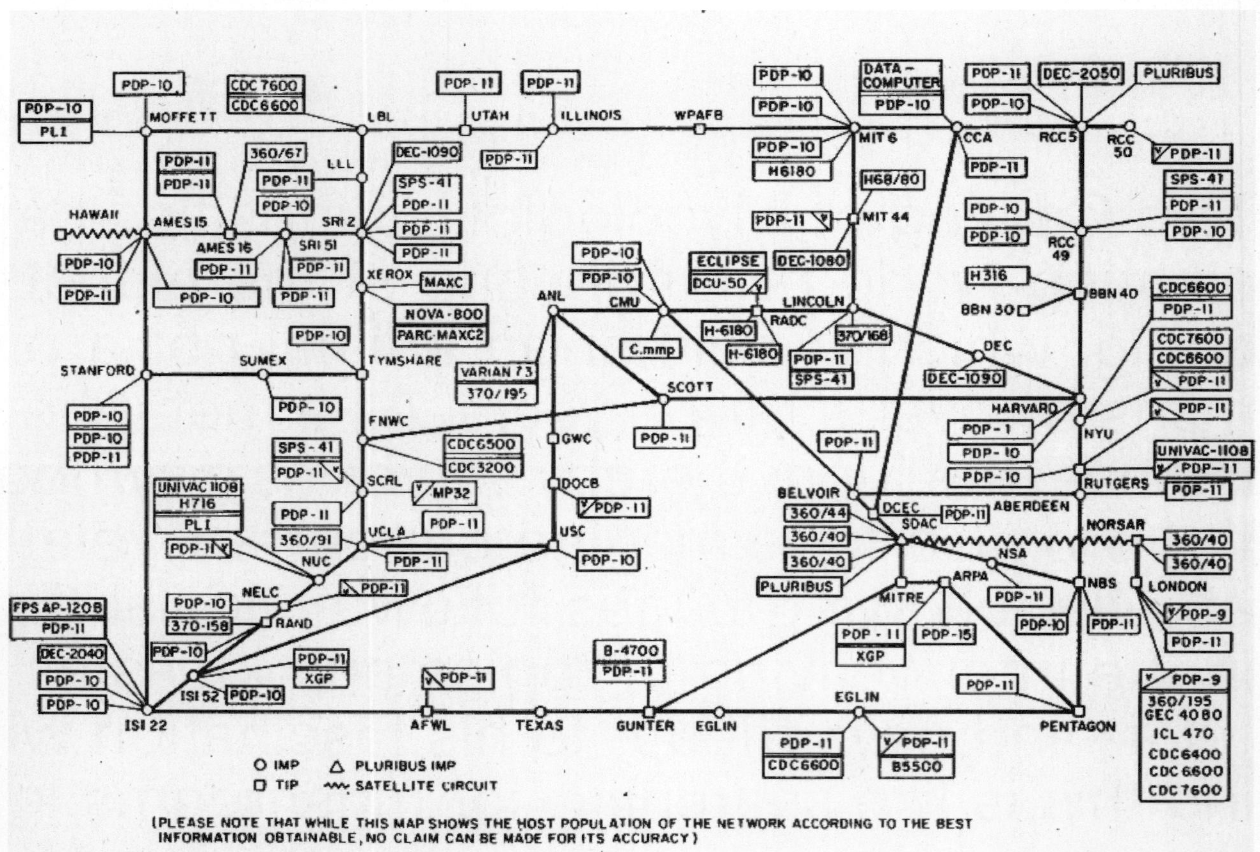

Sketch of the ARPANET logical map circa 1977

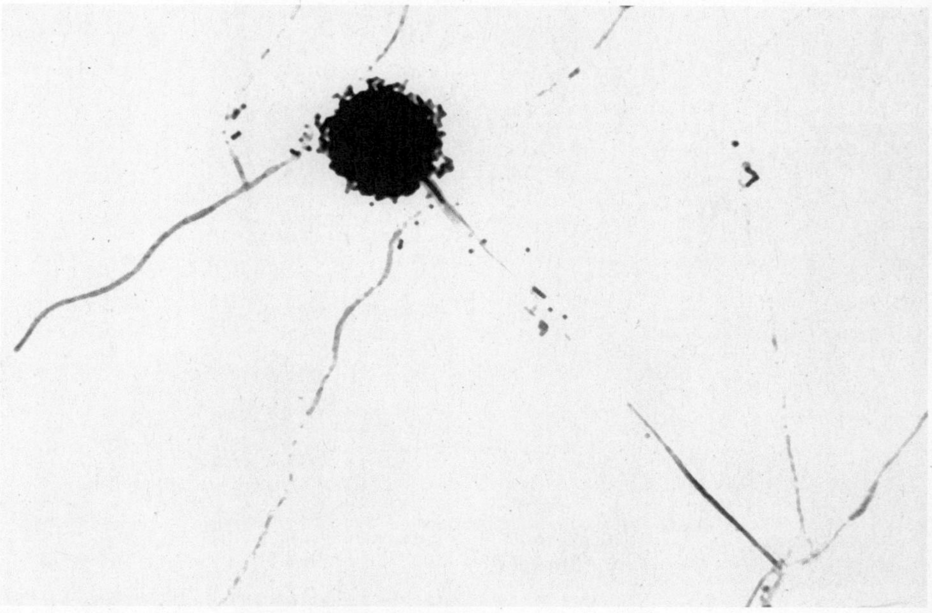

Photomicrograph of the head of the fungi Aspergillus niger

Aspergillus fungus

The genus Aspergillus was first named in 1729 by Italian priest and biologist Pier Antonio Micheli because of its shape that, under the microscope, reminded him of an aspergillum, holy water sprinkler.
There are around few hundred Aspergillus mould species found in a wide variety of environments and some can be occasionally harmful to humans and animals. Over the past two decades, the search for finding alternatives to chemical process in industrial production has highlighted the degrading-properties of the enzymes produced by the fungal genus Aspergillus.
A large number of these enzymes have already found commercial application, from food industries to textiles and leather industries.
Credit: CDC/Dr. Lucille K. Georg (PHIL #3964), 1955;
Source: Wikimedia Commons

Beatrix Potter

Aside from being the worldwide successful author of *The Tale of Peter Rabbit*, source of inspiration for Maurice Sendak's illustrations and George Orwell's masterwork *Animal Farm*, British author and illustrator Beatrix Potter (1866–1943) was at first place a natural scientist and a mushrooms expert.
Potter's first known watercolours of mushrooms date from the summer of 1887, when she was twenty years old. She would go on to produce some 350 highly accurate pictures of fungi, mosses and spores, collecting mushroom specimens herself and mounting them for careful observation under the microscope.
Unfortunately during her life Potter received no recognition for her discoveries because of her being a woman, but yet to this days her fungi illustrations and research are considered valuable by mycologists all over the world.
Lepiota friesii;
credit: Armitt Museum;
Source: britmycolsoc.org.uk
Hygrocybe punicea; Credit: Armitt Museum;
Source: britmycolsoc.org.uk

Beatrix Potter's watercolour of Hygrocybe punicea, also called a scarlet waxy cap, that she collected in October 1894

Specimen of Trichoderma Fungi

Bioremediation

Fungi have been proven to be a very efficient, cost-effective, and eco-friendly way for helping to remove a wide array of toxins from damaged environments or wastewater. This has been proven by an impressive experiment carried by mycologist Paul Stamets, who succeeded in making a diesel-contaminated area fertile again. By adding *Pleurotus ostreatus* mushroom spawn on one of the pile of contaminated soil, the findings demonstrated that the contamination had gone from 20,000 parts per million to a shocking 200 parts per million after only eight weeks, bringing back plants and animal life.
Author: AJC1;
Source: Wikimedia Commons

Biofuel

Fungi probably have received the least attention, positive or negative, in the biofuel arena. But recent studies have demonstrated that several types of fungi may actually make it easier and more efficient to produce biofuels from plant feedstock. According to the Clean Technologies and Environmental Policy Journal, certain species of the fungi Trichoderma have the power to break down waste crops into sugars and turn it into useful ethanol fuel.
Author: Keisotyo;
Source: Wikimedia Commons

Specimen of Oyster Mushroom, Pleurotus Ostreatus

Photo of the installation *MycoTree*, a structure made from mushroom mycelium and bamboo at the Seoul Biennale of Architecture and Urbanism, 2017

Brick

A mycelium brick is formed from organic waste and the mycelium of fungi. This hundred-percent organic material has been gradually developed across multiple disciplines, with the architectural and construction industry recently taking interest in its possible implications. For example, architects Felix Heisel and Dirk E. Hebel of ETH Zürich make bricks of mushroom material with good insulating properties, which are slightly heavier than polystyrene and whose texture resembles that of wood chipboard. Its production consumes hardly any energy and biodegrades after use.
Credit: Carlina Teteris;
Source: mycote.ch

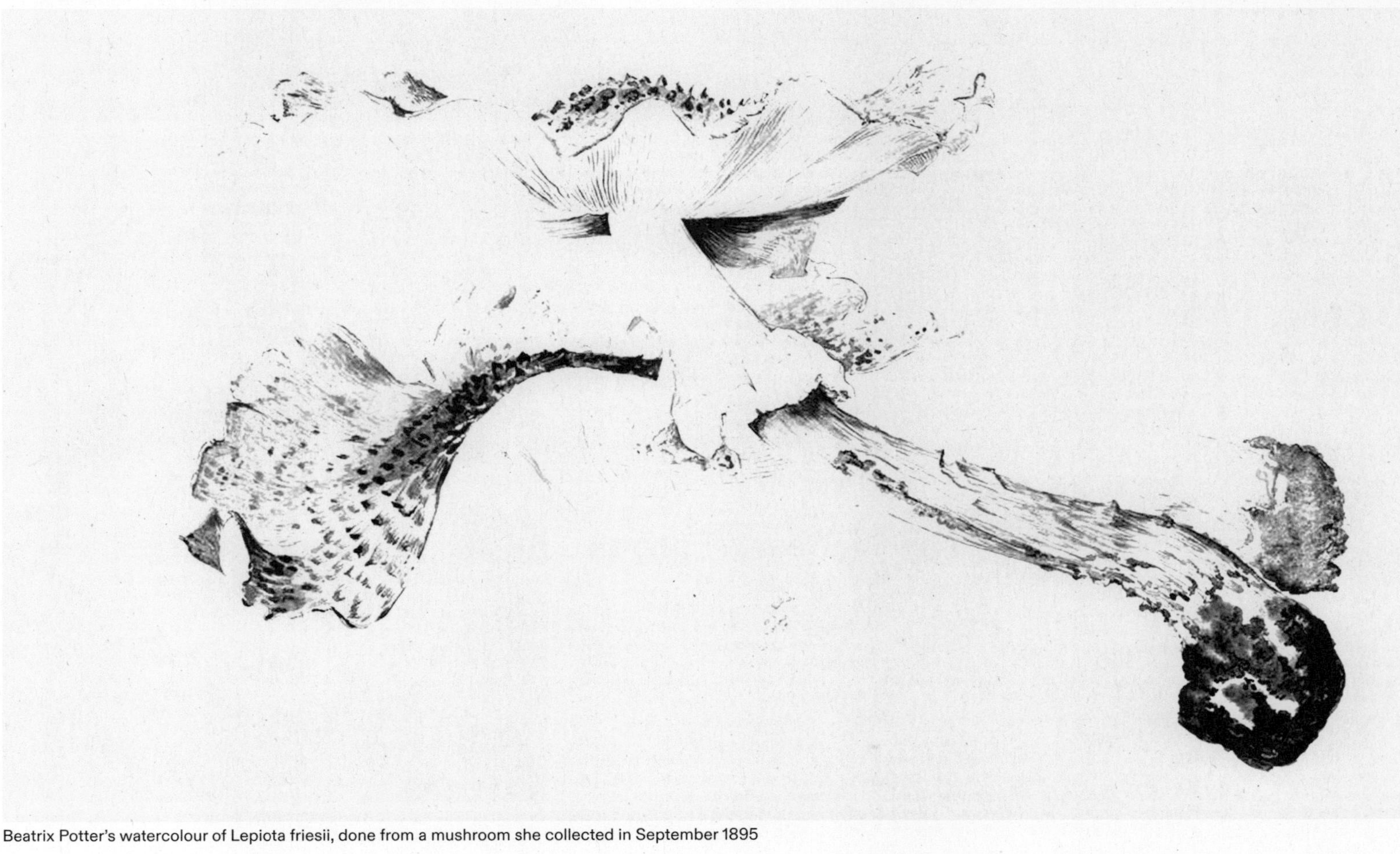

Beatrix Potter's watercolour of Lepiota friesii, done from a mushroom she collected in September 1895

Photo of Carsten Höller's installation *Soma* at Hamburger Bahnhof, Berlin, 2000

Photo of Carsten Höller's installation *Upside Down Mushroom Room* at Fondazione Prada Torre, Milano, 2000

Carsten Höller

Contemporary celebrated artist Carsten Höller researches new possibilities for perceiving existence through a method of rigorous investigation that recalls his scientific training.
One of his favourite subjects are mushrooms, which have been regularly featured in his work since 1994. In particular the artist's interest in the phenomenological and psychoactive properties of Amanita muscaria is visible in many of his installations, including the Mushroom Suitcase series, the *Upside Down Mushroom Room* or the Giants Triple Mushrooms three-dimensional collages.

Another one is the fantastical scenario filled with reindeers, mice, canaries, and a mushroom-shaped "floating hotel" that Höller created in 2010 for SOMA at Hamburger Bahnhof Berlin. In this three-dimensional tableau vivant he explores the myth of "soma," the drink used in Indian Vedic culture to access the divine sphere hypothetically linked to fly-agaric mushroom effects.

Photo: Delfino Sisto Legnani and Marco Cappelletti; Source: Fondazione Prada
Soma; Credit: dpa/DPAS; Source: Welt.de

Casa a Fungo

From the visionary mind of architect and engineer Mario Cavallé, eight concrete igloo homes and two mushroom-shaped houses have sprung up in the Maggiolina neighbourhood, Milan, in 1946. Cavallè's residential experiment served to accommodate the middle class left homeless after the allied bombing that took place in Milan in 1944. The fifty square meters extravagant residency were inspired by the circular housing model widespread in the US at the time. Twenty years later, the

Photo of a *Mushroom house* designed by Architect Mario Cavallé for the Maggiolina neighbourhood, Milan

mushrooms houses were destroyed but Via Lepanto is still known as the gnomes street.
Author: Anonymous;
Source: Wikimedia Commons

Controlled Substances Act

In 1970 US president Richard Nixon introduced the Controlled Substances Act as part of his "War on Drugs," to regulate the manufacture and distribution of most psychoactive drugs.
Under this statute magic mushrooms, among other substances, were made illegal. In 1994, Nixon's domestic policy advisor John Ehrlichman openly admitted that the criminalization of various narcotics, stimulants, depressants, and hallucinogens, were an overt attempt to vilify antiwar left and black people. "Did we know we were lying about the drugs? "Of course we did"—he declared in an interview conducted by journalist Dan Baum.
Source: Quartz

Photo of Richard Nixon seated with his domestic policy advisor, John Ehrlichman

Cretaceous Period

About 65.5 million years ago, nearly all large vertebrates and many tropical invertebrates became extinct in what was clearly a geological, climatic and biological event with worldwide consequences. The event was formally known as the Cretaceous-Tertiary (K-T) and marked the boundary between the Cretaceous and Paleogene Periods. Recent careful studies of some well-preserved material demonstrated that fungi and other saprophytes, which live on dead organisms, must have been the dominating life form on Earth.
Credit: Karla Bertram;
Source: berkeley.edu/fungi/fungifr.htm

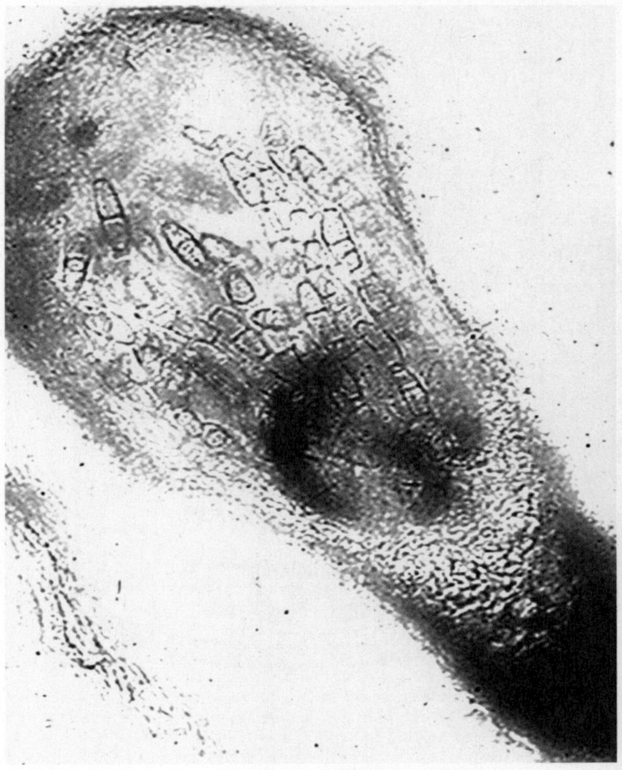

Photo of fossilized perithecium of what is believed to be a fungus of the genus Savoryella

Dark Taxa

A growing proportion of fungal species and lineages are known only from sequence data and cannot be linked to any physical specimen or resolved taxonomic name. Such fungi are often referred to as "dark taxa" or "dark matter fungi". As they lack a taxonomic identity in the form of a name, they are regularly ignored in many important contexts, for example in legalisation and species counts. Only 56 types of fungi have been evaluated for the IUCN Red List, compared with more than 25,000 plants and 68,000 animals.

Eat

Eat is an art experiment created by Andy Warhol in 1963 as part of the trilogy of so called 'anti-films' Sleep, Eat, Kiss. This 35-minute silent black and white film depicts fellow pop artist Robert Indiana engaged in the process of slowly eating some mushrooms for the entire length of the film.
Source: The Andy Warhol Museum

Still from the Andy Warhol's film *Eat*, 1964

Embrodery

Award winning textile designer Amanda Cobbett creates realistic three-dimensional papier-mâché and machine-embroidered sculptures of fungi, moss, lichen and bark, that she observes during her daily walks in the forest. Machining approximately 130,000 individual stitches a day, her creations highlighting the beauty and diversity that exists in the undergrowth.
Credit: Fraser James.
Source: textileartist.com

Photo of Orange Birch Bolete, a three-dimensional papier mache and embroidered sculpture by the textile artist Amanda Cobbett, 2019

Cover for *Everything under a Mushroom* illustrated by Margot Tomes, 1973

Everything under a Mushroom

In *Everything under a Mushroom*, every double-page spread carries a large picture of a mushroom under which are listed in rhyming texts a variety of activities and all the little things that can fit under a mushroom.
Source: Amazon

Extraterrestrial

Eclectic American writer, philosopher, and ethnobotanist Terence McKenna was a pioneer of the believe that mushrooms did not originated on Earth. In his 1989 book *True Hallucinations* McKenna expands on his so called theory of the "Martian Mushroom" that foresees the ability for the mushroom spores to survive space travel to become the catalyst of human evolution.
In McKenna's words: "Star- traveling species could be presumed to have a sophisticated knowledge of genetics and DNA function and therefore would not necessarily bear the form that evolution on a native planet had given them. They might well look as they wished to look. The mushroom, with its habit of living off nonliving

Front cover for Terence McKenna's *True Hallucinations*, 1989

organic matter and its cobweb-fragile underground network of ephemeral mycelium, seems an organism designed with Buddhist values of noninterference and low environmental impact in mind."
Source: Amazon

rings ever found is near Belfort in France. Formed by *Infundibulicybe geotropa*, it is thought to be about 600 metres in diameter and over 700 years old.
A Fairy Ring. Source: Unknown
Photo of a mushroom ring in the woods. Credit: Alison Chaiken; Source: Flickr

offered by the fungi kingdom for urgent medical and environmental questions, highlighting the their fundamental role for the survival of the entire ecosphere
Source: *The New York Times*

Photo of a mushroom ring in the woods

Still from Michelangelo Antonioni's *L'Eclisse*, with Monica Vitti, in the film Vittoria, walking near the Fungo-Eur and a torn-up vacant lot, 1962

Painting *A Fairy Ring* by Walter Jenks Morgan (1847-1924)

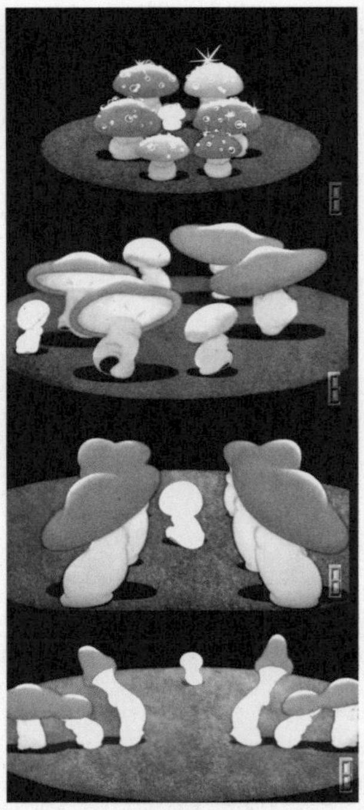

Screenshots *The Mushroom Dance's* clip from the movie *Fantasia*, 1940

Fairy Ring

The term "fairy ring" defines the naturally occurring ring or arc of mushrooms. Also known as fairy circle, elf ring, or pixie ring, this natural manifestation is associated with a considerably body of folklore. People once believed that mushrooms growing in a circle followed the path made by fairies dancing or they were thought to delimit the witches' dancing on Walpurgis Night, according to German tradition. One of the largest

Fantastic Fungi

The 2009 film *Fantastic Fungi* is a scientific exploration and visual journey through the fascinating, little-known realm of fungi, directed by cinematographer and producer Louie Schwartzberg, notable for his time-lapse of nature.
The film explores through the eyes of outstanding mycologists and authors like Paul Stamets, Michael Pollan, Eugenia Bone, Andrew Weil and others, the uses and benefits

Fantasia

Released for the first time in 1940, Fantasia is a milestone Walt Disney's experimental movie that animates eight segments of well-regarded classical music compositions. The conceptual framework of the individual pieces embraces such areas as prehistoric times, the four seasons, the opposition between light and darkness and classical mythology. One of the most well known passages of the film features six red-topped dancing mushrooms evolving in Chinese men choreographed into a Chinese Dance sequence, following the notes of Tchaikovsky's *The Nutcracker Suite*.
Source: Youtube

Fungo-Eur

Fungo [Mushroom] is a striking 50 metres high structure high that rises in EUR suburb in Rome. Begun by the Fascist regime in the late 1930s to celebrate the 20th anniversary of the March on Rome in 1922, once it was completed in 1960 it functioned as water tower with a restaurant on top. Michelango Antonioni's black and white drama *L'Eclisse* (1962), presents the Fungo as a symbol of alienation.
Source: researchgate.net

Untitled [Golden Mushroom] from *Campbell's Soup II*. Screenprint on paper. 1969

Screenshot from Louie Schwartzberg's documentary *Fantastic Fungi*, 2009

Golden Mushroom

The 1969 *Golden Mushroom's* screen print is part of Andy Warhol's *Campbell's Soup II* series, among the most recognised images of American modern art. Warhol's inspiration for the series developed from his personal life, as he explained in an interview with Gene Swenson in 1963—"I used to drink it [Campbell's soup cans]. I used to have the same lunch every day, for twenty years, I guess, the same thing over and over again." Repetition, appropriation and mass production's depiction would become the signature of Andy Warhol's art.
Credit: Gift of Dr. and Mrs. Herbert W. Johnson, 1993; Source: © The Andy Warhol Foundation for the Visual Arts / ARS, New York

Growing Lab

Officina Corpuscoli, founded in 2010 by designer and researcher Maurizio Montalti, is a trans-disciplinary studio based in Amsterdam that investigates how fungal organisms can be used to transform the current consumption-oriented economic system into a more eco-friendly and self-sustaining society. *Growing Lab* is one of the ongoing design-research project carried by Montalti to explore

Photo of the mycelium-based products produced at the *Growing Lab*

and assess methodologies for the implementation of mycelium-based materials as alternative to traditional synthetic (oil-based), toxic materials, such as plastics.
Source: Officina Corpuscoli

Impressions de la Haute Mongolie

Impressions de la Haute Mongolie is a surrealist film directed in 1975 by Salvador Dalí in collaboration with José Montes-Baquer, tribute to the French writer Raymond Roussel's novel Impressions d'Afrique (1910). The 50-minute unique audio-visual is an imaginary journey that revolves around the story of a Mongol princess who feeds her subjects powdered mushrooms, which produce hallucinations and stimulate them to paint. A scientific expedition is sent to Upper Mongolia in search of the mysterious giant hallucinogenic, unknown in the West.
Source: Youtube

Still from Salvador Dali's Impressions de la Haute Mongolie, 1975

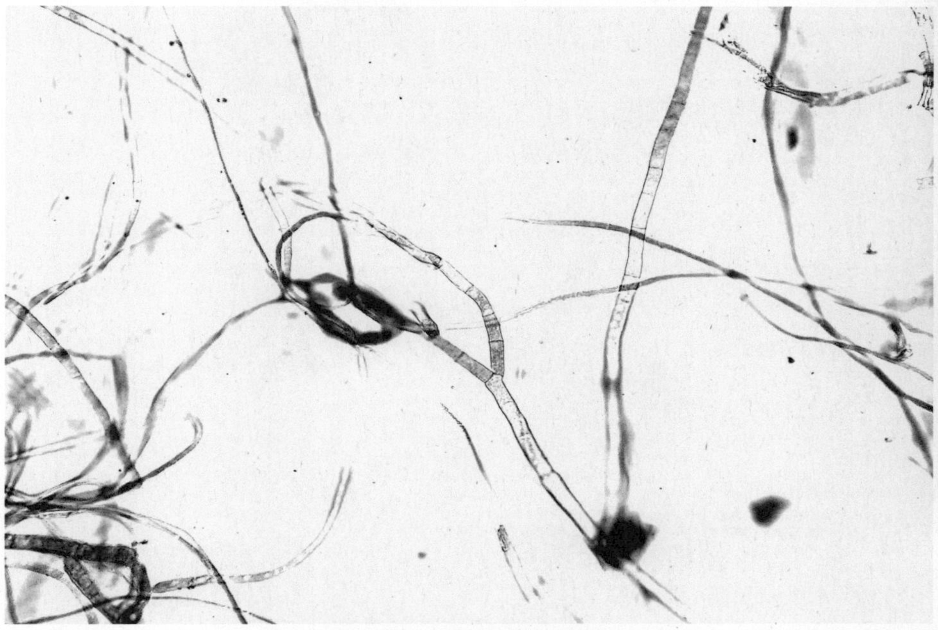

Microscopic photo of fungal hyphae stained by lactophenol cotton blue

Hypha

A hypha (plural: hyphae), from the Greek ὑφή, huphḗ, "web," is the thread-like filament that makes up a multicellular fungus and it is responsible for its growth. Hyphae are associated with multiple function, including the release of enzymes for the absorption and transportation of nutrients from food sources.
Author: Microrao;
Source: Wikimedia Commons

Hy-Fi

Hy-Fi is the organic mushroom-brick tower designed by New York City architecture firm The Living for the MoMa's Young Architects Contest in 2014. Twelve metres high and built from 10,000 living bricks, Hy-Fi is the first large scale structure to use innovative mushroom brick technology. This is the result of a collaboration between The Living and Ecovative, a company that has been growing bricks from mycelium and using them to replace typical plastic packaging material.
Credit: Image courtesy of MoMA PS1; photo: Kris Graves

Installation view of Hy-Fi by The Living at MoMA PS1, 2014

Infinity Burial Suit

Inspired by mushrooms as symbol and tool for a cultural shift to rethink the relationship with death and the planet, Jae Rhim Lee, artist and founder of the company Coeio, designed and developed a burial suit infused with fungal spores. Using her own hair, nails and skin cells, Lee developed the "Infinity Mushroom," a hybrid mushroom that can decompose bodies and metabolize toxins, turning corpses into nutrient-rich soil without harming the environment.
Source: Coeio.com

Model of Infinity Burial Suit

John Cage

Aside from being one of the 20th century most well-regarded artist and avant-garde composer, John Cage is something of a mushroom expert. In 1958 he won $10,000 in a quiz contest on Italian television for enumerating the 24 names of the white-spored Agaricus. In 1959, Cage further formalized his interest in mushrooms-identification by teaching a class on the discipline at the New School in New York City and three years later he co-founded the New York Mycological Society. In the 1960s, Cage was regularly supplying New York restaurants with the pickings from his mushroom hunts and in 1972 he published in collaboration with the mycologist Alexander H. Smith and the artist Lois Long the Mushroom Book, filling the pages with more recipes, poems, scattered observations, diary entries, and illustrations of mushrooms.
"I have come to the conclusion that much can be learned about music by devoting oneself to the mushroom"– Cage explained in Music Lovers' Field Companion (1954).
Source: Boreas Fine Art

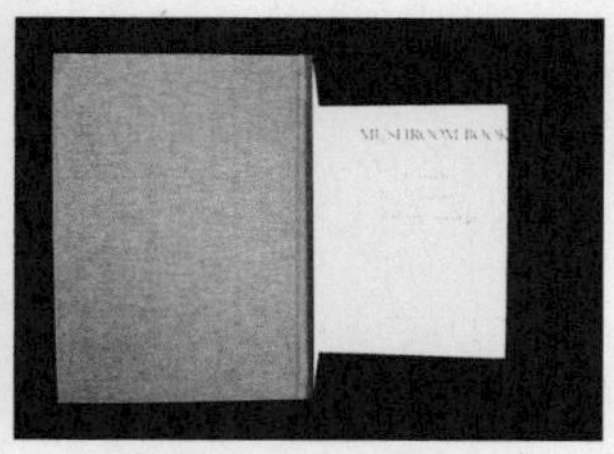

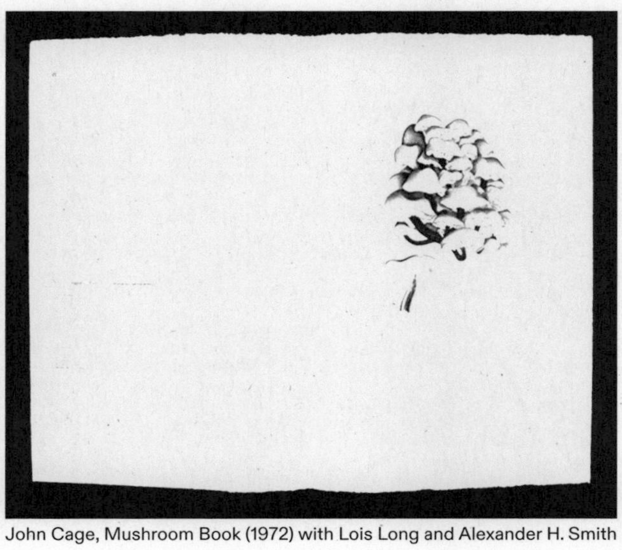

John Cage, Mushroom Book (1972) with Lois Long and Alexander H. Smith

Kingdom Fungi

Fungi is any of about 144,000 known species of eukaryotic organisms, which includes yeasts, rusts, smuts, mildews, molds, and mushrooms. Fungi constitute a separate kingdom, despite for long time they have been wrongly associate with the kingdom plant, and are among the most widely distributed organisms on Earth encompassing an enormous biodiversity, which ranges from unicellular aquatic chytrids to large mushrooms. Their taxonomy is based mainly on morphology and physiology, following the 17th century pioneering work of Carl Linnaeus (1707–1778) among others, but recent phylogenetic studies have challenged the historical groupings and reshaped the classification within Kingdom Fungi. The study of fungi is known as mycology, from the Greek mykes "mushroom" and logos "discourse."
Source: Alchetron

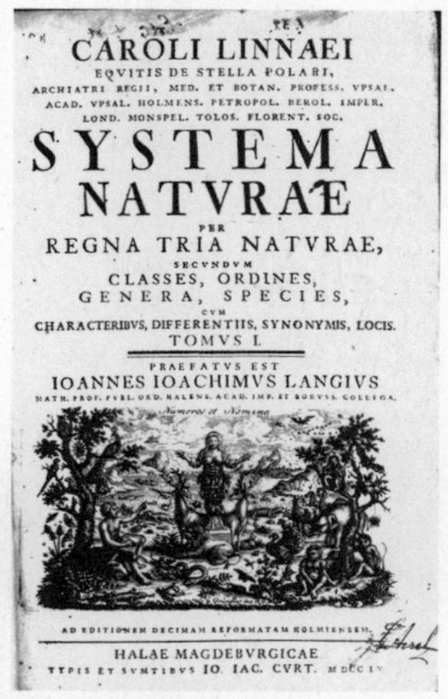
CAROLI LINNAEI
EQUITIS DE STELLA POLARI,
SYSTEMA
NATVRAE
PER
REGNA TRIA NATVRAE,
SECUNDUM
CLASSES, ORDINES,
GENERA, SPECIES,
CUM
CHARACTERIBUS, DIFFERENTIIS, SYNONYMIS, LOCIS.
TOMUS I.
PRAEFATUS EST
IOANNES IOACHIMUS LANGIUS
HALAE MAGDEBURGICAE

Cover of the 10th edition of the Systema Naturae by Carl Linnaeus, 1758

Close up of Reishi vegan leather's structure by MycoWorks

Leather

The aversion to the traditional leather industry and the desire to minimise its environmental impact have pushed several companies to experiment with leather substitute made out of fungi. Muskin, Mylo, Zoa, Reishi, are few names of more environmentally friendly vegan leather growth from mycelias cell. San Francisco-based startup MycoWorks is confident that by the year 2020 a fungus based leather substitute could be produced in adequate quantities for mass consumption.
Photography: Laura Gutierrez;
Source: MycoWorks

Les Schtroumpfs

Les Schtroumpfs [The Smurfs] is a Belgian comic franchise from 1958 created by cartoonist Peyo, pseudonym of Pierre Culliford, that narrates the adventures of a fictional colony of around hundred small, blue, human-like creatures who live in mushroom-shaped houses in the forest.
The Smurfs' community takes the form of a cooperative, based on the principle that each Smurf contribute to the Smurf society according to their skills. Symbol of the Smurfs is their phrygian caps, which came to represent freedom during the modern era.
Author: Peyo;
Source: wallpaper safari

Illustration of the Smurfs' village, 2006

Photo of Dr. Albert Hofmann doing Tai Chi movement with a Cubensis Mushroom in his right hand

LSD

In 1943 chemist Albert Hofmann discovered the hallucinogenic properties of the lysergic acid, a chemical from the ergot fungi. In the 1950s and early 1960s Lysergic Acid Diethylamide (LSD) was sold as a medication for research purposes under the trade-name Delysid before falling under restrictions of the Drug Abuse Control Amendment of 1965. During the mid-1960s, use of LSD spread widely in the emerging hippie counterculture and the shapes and colours characteristic of LSD-induced trips appear frequently in the visual art of the period. The drug also powerfully shaped the popular music of the Sixties and encouraged the mystical experimentation of those years.
Credit: Christian Rätsch

Mario Bros.

Mario Bros is a franchise game created by game designer Shigeru Miyamoto and produced in 1983 by Japanese video game company Nintendo, starring character Mario portrayed as an Italian plumber who resides in the fictional word of Mushroom Kingdom. His mission is to rescue Princess Toadstool (later known as Princess Peach) of the Mushroom Kingdom from King Koopa. Since Super Mario Bros. series, Magic Mushrooms—the most iconic from the Mushroom power-ups—are featured in the game to turn the protagonist Marion in Super Mario. With more than 600 million units sold worldwide, the overall Mario franchise is the best-selling video game franchise of all time.
Source: Vice

A screenshot from the original Super Mario Bros, 1985

Cover of the book "The Mushroom at the End of the World" by Anna Lowenhaupt Tsing, 2015

Matsutake

By investigating Matsutake mushrooms' globalised commodity chain—one of the world's most sought-after fungi—anthropologist Anna Lowenhaupt Tsing presents in her book *The Mushroom at the End of the World* an original examination into the relation between capitalist destruction and collaborative survival within multi-species landscapes.
The matsutake, from being a symbol of the Japanese elite during the Edo period, became embedded in the global commodity exchange networks as luxury product, symbolic of Japanese identity. Peculiar of this mushroom is the fact that it refuses to be cultivated but it thrives best in pines forest, where the soil is poor often due to human-induced degradation.
By examining this landscape, the precarity of people's lives involved in matsutake's foraging and trading, Tsing illustrates the economical forces that rules the capitalistic world.
The Mushroom at the End of the World; Source: Amazon

Illustration of matsutake from Minakata Kumagusu's Kinrui Zufu

Mayan Mushroom Stones

Miniature statues found in Guatemala present visual evidences that both the hallucinogenic Amanita muscaria and Psilocybin mushroom were worshiped and venerated as gods in ancient Mesoamerican cultures around 1000 B.C. The representation of those sacred mushrooms were so cleverly encoded in the religious art of Mesoamerica to escape detection and thus surviving the concerted efforts of Catholic missionaries to destroy any symbol not related to Christianity during the 16th century.
Author: Dr Richard Rose
reproduced from Stamets, 1996;
Source: mushroomstone.com

Mushroom stones discovered in Maya ruins of Kaminaljuyu, Guatemala

Medicinal fungi

Cultures around the world have used mushrooms in medicine since ancient time. Around 450 BCE Greek physician Hippocrates had already identified the properties of the Amadou mushroom for reducing inflammation and cauterizing wounds whilst in Chinese medicine Reishi's healing reputation was already stated in the Shen Nong Ben Cao Jing, the Chinese great classic herbal text written between about 200 and 250 CE.
There are no clinical evidence today on whether mushrooms help prevent or treat disease in humans, but mycologist and professor of biology David Hibbett reminds that

Illustration of a Chinese sage contemplating Ling-chih, the Divine Mushroom

from fungi derive some of our most important drugs, as for the cases of penicillin and cholesterol-lowering statins.
Author: Chen Hung-shou (1599–1652);
Source: Wikimedia Commons

The bombing of Hiroshima and Nagasaki, Japan, respectively the 6th and 9th August 1945, was described by the The Times of London as a "huge mushroom of smoke and dust", soon becoming the icon of the nuclear era that would represent both power and destruction and created a new consciousness of the globe as a single, interconnected entity.
Gerhard Vieth's *Physikalischer Kinderfreund*, 1798;
Source: Wikimedia Commons
Mushroom cloud above Nagasaki;
Source: Wikimedia Commons

Mushroom in the Rain

This children's book published in 1990 and written by prolific author and translator Mirra Ginsburg, narrates the story of a rain-soaked ant that seeks refuge under a mushroom. Page after page the mushroom will expand to shelter all its animal friends. The book happily remind us that mushrooms grow when it rains, with the the last double-page closeup full of orange, yellow, pink, violet, blue and green fungi's illustrations.
Author: Jose Aruego and Ariane Dewey;
Source: archive.org

Mushroom Town

English artist and author George Oliver Onions (1872–1961) is credited as one of the most important figures in the development of the psychological thriller. Awarded the James Tait Black Memorial Prize for his 1946 novel Poor Man's Tapestry, in the classic novel Mushroom Town Onions puts his keen eye for detail to work in a loving portrait of a fictionalized village in Wales.
Source: archive.org

Cover for G.Oliver Onion's *Mushroom Town*, 1946

Mushroom Wars

Initially released in 2009 for Sony PlayStation 3 Mushroom Wars is a real-time strategy video game developed by Creat Studios which became one of the RTS-genre pioneers critically acclaimed all around the world. Aim of the game is to increase the size of the Mushroom Army by opposing capturing villages and overwhelming the defending forces.
Source: mushroomwars.com

Mycelium

Mycelium or mycelia indicates the vegetative part of a fungus, consisting of a network of fine white filaments called hyphae. Observed under a microscope, mycelia can look like little trees before fruiting bodies mature, and it comes in many sizes, from very tiny to as large as a forest. Thanks to their rigid cell walls mycelia provides nutrition to the mushroom and are of vital importance in terrestrial and aquatic ecosystems for their role in the decomposition of organic compounds.
Author: Rob Hille;
Source: Wikimedia Commons

Cover for Mirra Ginsburg's *Mushroom in the Rain*, 1990

Still from the *Mushroom Wars* video game, 2009

Mushroom

Mushroom indicates the fleshy, umbrella-shaped fruiting body—also called sporophore—of certain fungi, typically of the agaric family. Even though there is no scientific distinction, the term mushroom commonly refers to the edible sporophore while toadstool is often used to indicate inedible or poisonous mushrooms. Most probably the word mushroom derives from the late Middle English adaptation of the Old French mousseron and adopted as verb in 19th century to signify the action of "spreading out".
Author: Nathan Wilson.
Source: Wikimedia Commons

Specimen of Agaricus Campestri, commonly known as mushroom

Mushroom cloud

"Mushroom cloud" describes a large cloud of smoke, flame and debris resulting from a big explosion, reminiscent of a mushroom in shape. The term appears to have been officially coined at the start of the 1950s even though this phenomena was already illustrated in Gerhard Vieth's *Physikalischer Kinderfreund* (1798).

Mushroom cloud in an engraving from Gerhard Vieth's *Physikalischer Kinderfreund*, 1798

Mushroom cloud above Nagasaki after atomic bombing on August 9, 1945

Photo of mycelium of *Agaricus bisporus*

Mycelium chair

Photo of *Mycelium Chair* by Studio Klarenbeek & Dros, 2018

Studio Klarenbeek&Dros are the first in the world to 3D-print living mycelium, the root structure of mushrooms, thanks to the technology developed since 2011 that makes possible to combine the threadlike network of fungi with local land waste. The purpose is to bring together machine and nature to create a new material that could be used to create products with a negative carbon footprint. The 2018 Mycelium Chair, now part of the permanent collection of the Centre Pompidou, is the first archetype object that shows the high potential for this technology to be implemented in a broad spectrum of application.
Source: ericklarenbeek.com

Front cover for *Mycelium Running* written by Paul Stamets, 2005

Logo of Stanford-Brown-RISD Team that worked on developing habitats for Mars and the Moon through the use of fungal mycelium

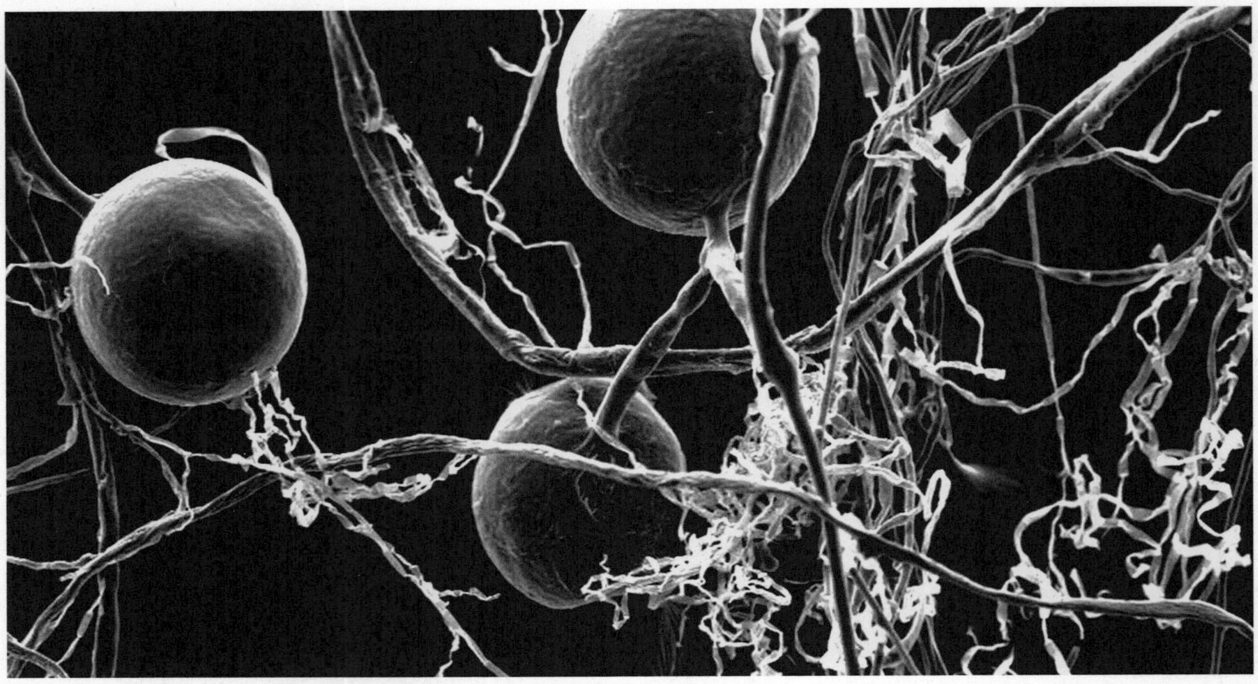
Photomicrograph of endomycorrhizal fungi with spores attached to the hyphal strands

Mycelium Running

Mycelium Running. How Mushrooms can help save the Planet by mycologist Paul Stamets is a pioneering text on the uses and applications of fungi in bioremediation. This manual unveils new methods for growing mushrooms, medicinal and nutritional properties of mycelia, and species selections that could strengthen sustainability of habitats while providing a multitude of biological benefits.

Myco-Architecture Project

NASA is exploring technologies that could grow structures out of fungi for potential future homes in the stars, and perhaps lead to more sustainable ways of living on Earth as well. "Right now, traditional habitat designs for Mars are like a turtle—carrying our homes with us on our backs—a reliable plan, but with huge energy costs" said Lynn Rothschild, the principal investigator on the early-stage project. Ultimately the project envisions a future where human explorers can bring a compact habitat built out of a lightweight material with dormant fungi that will last on long journeys to places like Mars.

Logo of Stanford-Brown-RISD Team; Source: Igem 2018
Off-planet habitat; Photography: L. Rothschild; Credit: NASA
Myco-Architecture; Credit: NASA

Mycophobia

Mycophobia is the fear of mushrooms and it manifests itself with the reluctance to eat or touch mushrooms or other fungi. The term was first introduced in 1887 by British mychologist W.D. Hay, who claimed that the people of Britain were well known for being fearful of mushrooms and stayed away from them because of their fear of poisoning. But mycophobia dates back to the ancient Greeks, as demonstrated by poet of the 2nd century BCE Nicander of Colophon, who in his Alexipharmaca use these words to speak of mushrooms: "Let not the evil ferment of the soil injure a man; it will often swell up in his chest, at other times it will choke him, when it is fostered over the viper's coil deep in its lair, sucking up the monster's venom and the noxious breath from its mouth. This is the evil ferment which they call Fungi in general."

Credit: Bibliotheque Nationale, Paris.

Mycorrhiza

The term mycorrhiza, from Greek μύκης "fungus" and ῥίζα "root," was first coined by 19th-century German biologist Albert Bernard Frank to describe the symbiotic association between a fungus and a plant and its role in the plant's root system, the rhizosphere.
In a mycorrhizal association, which resembles to a mild form of parasitism, the fungus colonises the host plant's root tissues to receive nutrients. Around 90% of land plants are in mutually-beneficial relationships with fungi.

Source: www.gardenerspantry.ca/microorganisms/mycorrhizal-fungi.html

Mycotecture

This term indicates the practice pioneered by artist and teacher Philip Ross to grow fungal materials into the form of walls, arches, columns and other building components.
For Mycotecture he created blocks from the fungus Ganoderma lucidum, a mushroom traditionally valued in Asia for its health benefits and with the ability to digest and bind together smaller pieces of organic materials into a tightly bound structure. Though incredibly strong and durable, these blocks can readily be broken down with a range of benign processes and incorporated back into the world.

Photography: Philip Ross

Mycotex

Inspired by soft-bodied species capable of replicating themselves over and over again, fashion designer Aniela Hoitink developed Mycotex, a sustainable fabric made out of mycelium, the roots of mushroom. Her explorations resulted in a fungi dress

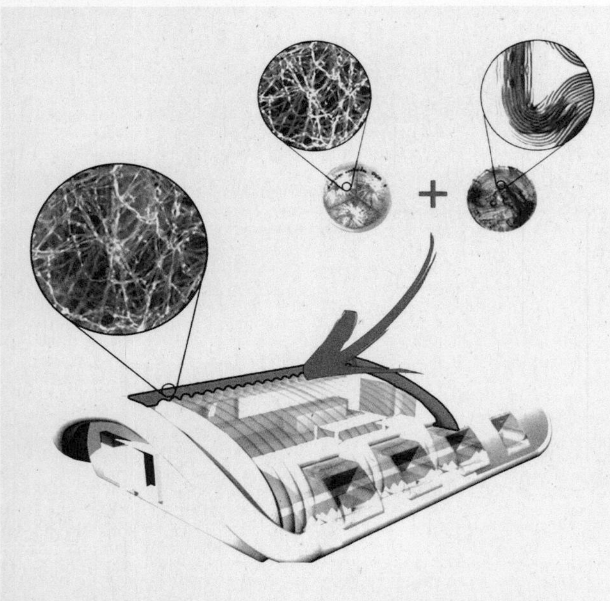
Graphic illustration of an off-planet habitat fabricated with fungi

Miniature from a 9th century codex (Grec 2179) of Dioscorides

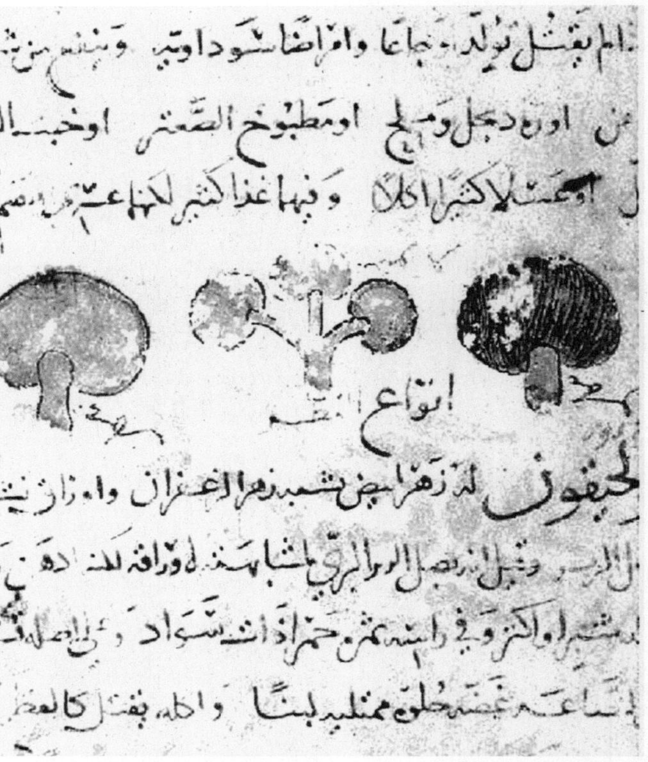
Miniature from a 11th century manuscript (Arabe 4947) of Dioscorides

Render of the concept Myco-Architecture developed by NASA

Photo of a building block grown from Ganoderma lucidum

Photo of a mycotecture arch built by Phil Ross

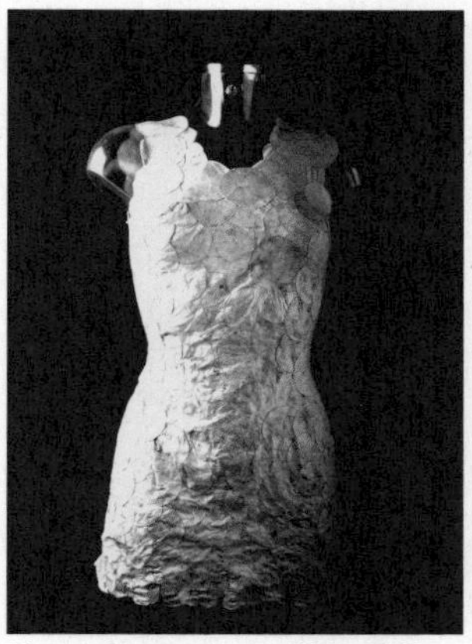

Photo of a prototype of MicoTEX fungi dress by Aniela Hoitink

which can be adjusted to adapt and repaired when needed. Once the garment is not in use anymore, it can be easily composted.
Source: neffa.nl

Natural History Part I

The two portfolios "Natural History Part I and Part II" made by American artist Cy Twombly are considered among the most important works of art of the mid-1970s. The first series "Natural History Part I" features scientific illustrations of mushrooms combined with notations, gestures and personal meditations. The prints, produced in 1974, can be read as allegories of mental structures and the human quest for knowledge.
Credit: © Cy Twombly Foundation; Source: tate.org.uk

New Mumbai

Tobias Revell's New Mumbai sci-fi documentary tells the story of the fungi that ended up hugging the walls of Dharavi slums of Mumbai, flooded with refugees looking to escape the conflict. The collective expertise of the refugees managed to turn genetically engineered fungal samples into a new type of infrastructure to supply heat, light and building material. Dharavi rapidly evolved its own micro-economy based around the mushrooms.
Source: tobiasrevell.com

Still from Tobias Revel's film *New Mumbay*, 2012

Nuclear Radiation

Radiotrophic fungi were discovered in 1991 growing inside and around the Chernobyl Nuclear Power Plant in Ukraine in the years since its 1986 meltdown. Researchers at the Albert Einstein College of Medicine in New York have demonstrated that fungi with a natural melanin shell—i.e. Cladosporium sphaerospermum, Wangiella dermatitidis, and Cryptococcus neoformans—use the pigment melanin to convert gamma radiation into chemical energy for growth. Aside from its role as an energy transporter, melanin also appears to confer a certain degree of radioresistance in radiotrophic fungi suggesting that these fungal species may have the ability to absorb and break down radioactive compounds in the environment.
Cryptococcus neoformans; author: CDC/Dr. Leanor Haley; Source: Wikimedia Commons
Chernobyl, Ukraine, 2019; credit: AP

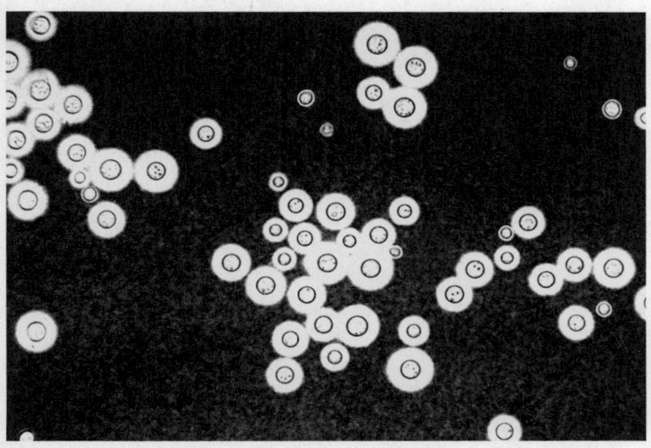

Micrograph of *Cryptococcus neoformans* using a light India ink staining preparation

Nutrition

Mycophagy, the act of consuming mushrooms, dates back as early as the Upper Palaeolithic Period as proven by the 2015 discovery of remains of Boletales mushroom order in the teeth of the "Red Lady"—a Magdalenian woman skeleton buried nearly 19,000 years ago in el Mirón, Spain. During the Classical Period mushrooms would gained the status of luxury product reserved only for Egyptian royalty and the rulers of Romans, which would called

View of the remains of the Chernobyl nuclear reactor power plant's Reactor No. 4 where in 1991 a black fungi was found sprouting on the walls, Chernobyl, Ukraine, 2019

Natural History, Part I: *Mushrooms, no. IV*, 1974. Lithograph and mixed media on paper

Photo of Egyptians crafted laws prohibiting commoners from eating mushrooms, 2500 BC ca. Author: George Shuklin

them "food of the Gods" (Niksic et al. 2015). Nowadays mushrooms popularity have increased drastically, with 2018 global mushroom market consumption of 12.74 million tons (MT) and projected to reach 20.84 million tons (MT) by 2026.

Licensed under Creative Commons Attribution-ShareAlike 3.0 Unported.

Octoshroom

Large mushroom-like organisms that live on Pandora—the fictional universe created for the James Cameron's movie *Avatar* released in 2009, inhabited by a sapient indigenous humanoid species called Na'vi. Octoshroom or Torukspxam meaning "last shadow fungus" in Na'vi language, describes bioluminescent and extremely toxic fungus that possesses a giant underground filament network that enable them to feed.

Credit: James Cameron, Avatar: An Activist Survival Guide; Source: Avatar Wikiw

Ophiocordyceps unilateralis

Ophiocordyceps genus belongs to a family of parasitic fungi that counts around 140 species with the ability to grow on insects.

One of the most cited parasite is the Ophiocordyceps unilateralis, also known as the zombie-ant fungus for its ability to take control of ants' behaviour, in particular of the tribe of campotini typical of tropical forest ecosystems. Once killed the insect, O. unilateralis propagates by growing its fruiting bodies from the ant's head and eventually releasing spores to start the cycle anew.

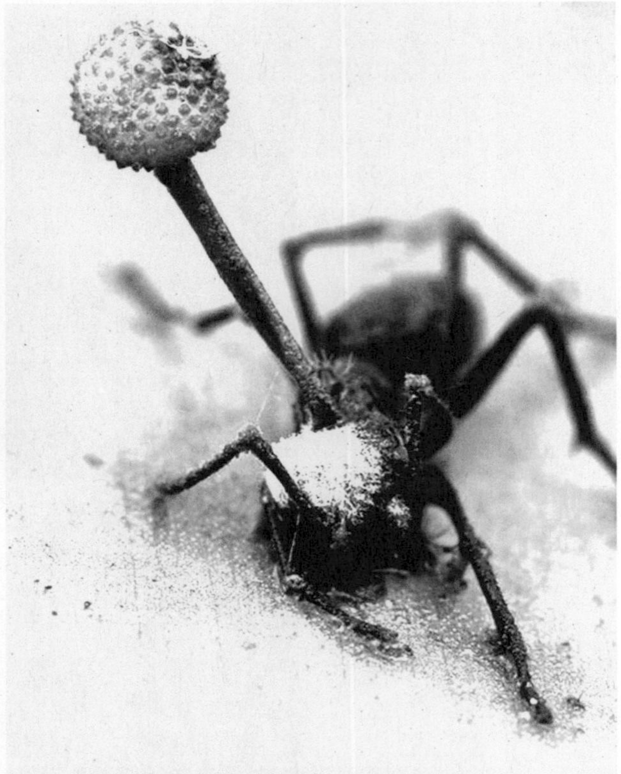

Photo of dead ants infected with Ophiocordyceps unilateralis

Photo of dried Piptoporus betulines fungus on a leather thong near Otzi's body

Ötzi

The 5,300 year-old and most well-preserved "Iceman" nicknamed Ötzi, discovered by hikers in the Italian Alps in September 1991, has been found with the fruiting body of Piptoporus betulines hanging on his leather band. It is believed Ötzi used this particular fungus as a medication to cure stomach and intestinal disorder.

Credit: wisthaler.com; Source: South Tyrol Museum of Archaeology

Outer Space / Kvant-2

In 1988, Russian cosmonauts noticed that something from outer space was growing on the outside window of the Mir-Kvant 2'module of the space station. Later Russian microbiologist Natalia Novikova determined that this living, pulsating, and corroding mass of tissue capable of eating the control panels and digesting the communications unit, were fungi. Fungi from space.

Indeed fungi proved to be adapted to living in the highly radioactive environment of space, which is 500 times that of Earth.

Author: NASA; Source: archive. org

Penicillin

Penicillin is one of the first and most widely used antibiotic agents derived from the Penicillium fungi mould. In 1928 Scottish bacteriologist Alexander Fleming first observed the antibacterial effect of penicillin in a Petri dish of his

Image of Octoshroom from James Cameron's movie *Avatar*, 2009

A survey of the Mir Space Station, viewed from the Orbiter Endeavour during STS-89 (DTO 1118), 1998

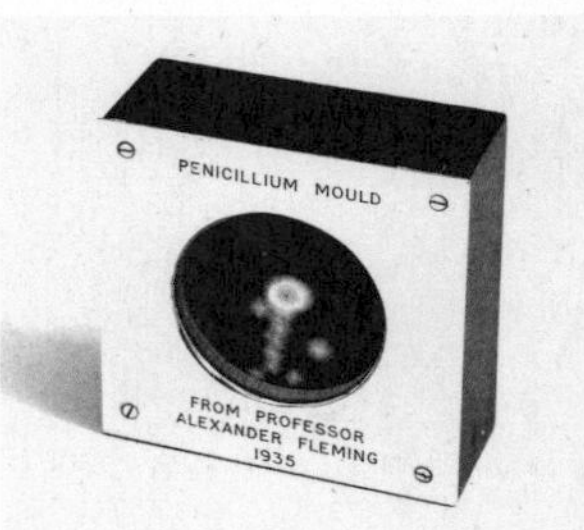

Sample of penicillium mould presented by Alexander Fleming to Douglas Macleod, 1935

laboratory. However was only in the 1940s, after Australian pathologist Howard Florey and British biochemist Ernst Boris Chain isolated and purified penicillin, that an injectable form of the drug was available for therapeutic use on an industrial scale. All three scientists shared the Nobel Prize for this work, and penicillin rapidly became the 'wonder drug' that marks a true turning point in medicine.
Source: Wikimedia Commons

Print of the slogan "Unity, Indivisibility of the Republic, Liberty, Equality, Fraternity or Death" of the First Republic of France surmounted by a phrygian cap, 1793

Phrygian cap

Phrygian cap is a soft conical cap characterised by a bent over apex worn in antiquity by the inhabitants of Phrygia, a region of central Anatolia.
Phrygian cap was probably mistaken for the pileus, the felt cap of emancipated slaves in ancient Rome, when it emerged as emblem of liberty during the French Revolution (1787–1799). By 1793, members of the Assemblies of Paris were obliged to wear "the red cap of liberty" and it continues to be associated with the national allegorical figure of Liberté.
Source: Wikimedia Commons

Plastic

The 2018 first-ever State of the World's Fungi report revealed the potential of Fungi to tackle plastic pollution. Scientists from Kew Garden, leading institutions for fungal research, highlighted the natural properties of Aspergillus tubingensis fungus to decompose plastic molecules far quicker than the decades it takes for the material to naturally disintegrate. First documented in 2017 on a rubbish dump in Pakistan, the Aspergillus tubingensis's ability to decompose plastic could be of a great help to combat the damage of our huge buildups of plastic waste.
Piece of plastic broken;
Photography: Sehroon Khan;
Source: guardian.com
Microschopic photography,
Photography: Sehroon Khan;
Source: research.gate

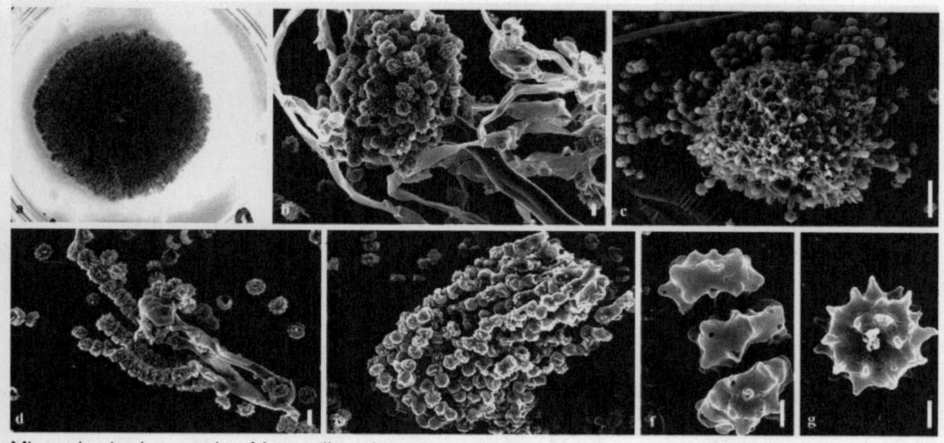

Microschopic photography of Aspergillus tubingensis culture

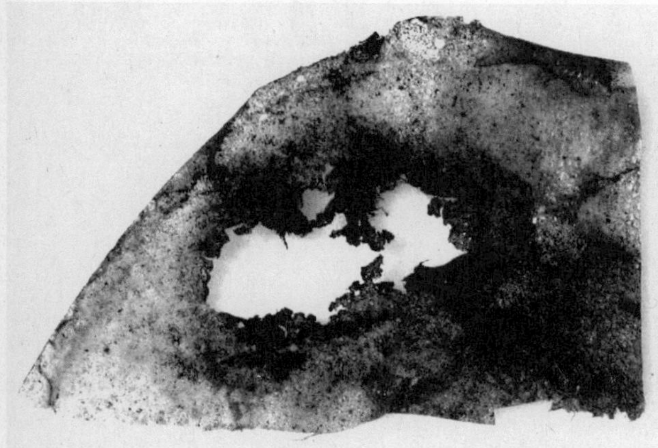

Photo of a piece of plastic broken down by Aspergillus tubingensis

Psilocybe semilanceata

Psilocybe semilanceata, commonly known as liberty cap for its resemblance to the Phrygian cap's symbol of liberty, is one of the most widely distributed mushroom containing the psychoactive compounds psilocybin and baeocystin. According to several studies aimed at quantified the hallucinogenic compounds levels, Psilocybe semilanceata is considered to be one of the most potent hallucinogenic mushroom in nature.
Specimens photographed in Sweden. Source: Wikipedia

Poem

Mushrooms is a poem written in 1959 by Sylvia Plath, considered one of the most admired and controversial of postwar poets writing in English.
Part of her first collection *The Colossus and Other Poems*, Mushrooms have been considered by scholars and readers to be a feminist allegory. Overnight, very Whitely, discreetly, Very quietly. Our toes, our noses. Take hold on the loam, Acquire the air. Nobody sees us, Stops us, betrays us; The small grains make room. Soft fists insist on Heaving

Cover of the first edition of *The Colossus and Other Poems* by Sylvia Plath, 1960

the needles, The leafy bedding, Even the paving. Our hammers, our rams, Earless and eyeless, Perfectly voiceless, Widen the crannies, Shoulder through holes. We Diet on water, On crumbs of shadow, Bland-mannered, asking Little or nothing. So many of us! So many of us! We are shelves, we are Tables, we are meek, We are edible, Nudgers and shovers In spite of ourselves. Our kind multiplies: We shall by morning Inherit the earth. Our foot's in the door.
Source: dominicwinter.co.uk

Illustration of Teonanacatl as represented by a 16th century Mexican artist

Teonanacatl, meaning "flesh of the Gods" in Nahuatl language.
It was from this species that Dr. Albert Hofmann, already known as "the father of LSD", isolated and named the active entheogenic compounds psilocybin and psilocin in the late 1950s.
Source: Magliabechiano Codex, Biblioteca Nazionale, Florence.

Radical Mycology

Radical Mycology is one of the most comprehensive books on mycology ever published, drawing on the 15 years of practice and study in the field of author Peter McCoy, co-founder of the grassroots organisation Radical Micology.
With step-by-step protocols, hundreds of photographs and illustrations, and over a dozen appendices dedicated to uniqueness of fungal biology, the critical ecological roles of micro and macro fungi, the importance of lichens as indicators of

Psilocybe mexicana

Psilocybe mexicana is a psychedelic mushroom first categorised in 1957 by French botanist Roger Heim, but already known by the natives of Central America and North America over 2,000 years ago. In particular Nahuatl people, also known as the Aztecs, had long history and a strong tradition related to the usage of Psilocybe mexicana and other mushrooms of the same Psilocybe genus. They would call them

Photo of the fruit bodies of the hallucinogenic mushroom Psilocybe semilanceata

Cover for Peter McCoy's *Radical Mycology*, 2016

Electron microscopy image of asexual apparatus of Aspergillus niger

environmental health, and the profound influences that fungi have held on the evolution of all life and human cultures, McCoy's book showcases the amazing power of mushrooms.

Reproduction

After a period of intensive growth, Fungi enter a reproductive phase by forming and releasing vast quantities of spores either floating on the wind or hitching a ride on an animal. Fungi can spread quickly through asexual reproduction when conditions are stable or, if the environment is changing, sexual reproduction can help them to increase their genetic variation and thus their chances to survive.

Credit: Read N. D., "Low-temperature scanning electron microscopy of fungi and fungus-plant interactions," pp. 17–29.
In: Mendgen K. and Lesemann D. (eds.) *Electron Microscopy of Plant Pathogens*, Springer-Verlag, Berlin, Germany, Copyright © 1991;
Source: oxfordmedicine.com

Rhizome

Rhizome is the philosophical concept developed by philosopher Gilles Deleuze and psychoanalyst Félix Guattari in their Capitalism and Schizophrenia project (1972–1980). The term rhizome describes the search for knowledge that allows for multiplicity and non-hierarchical orders which allows cross-connection in data representation and interpretation.

"[...] Any point of a rhizome can be connected to anything other, and must be"—they state in the 1980 book *Mille Plateaux*. The rhizomatic methodology, in contrast to the vertical and more linear tree-model which works with dualist categories and binary choices, makes visible what is often imperceptible.

Source: maggs.com

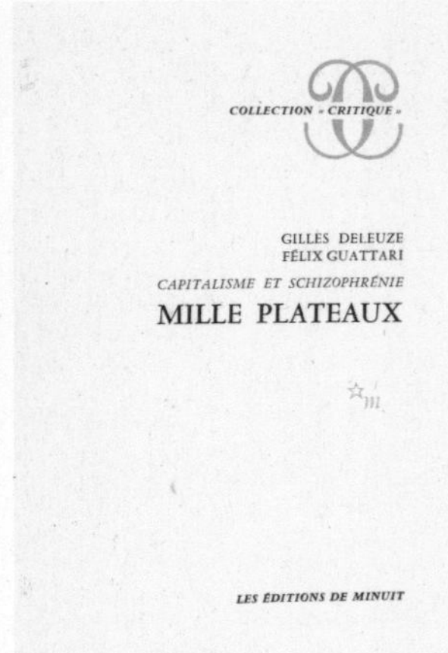

Cover for the first edition of Deleuze and Guattari's *Mille Plateaux*, 1980

Sacred Mushrooms

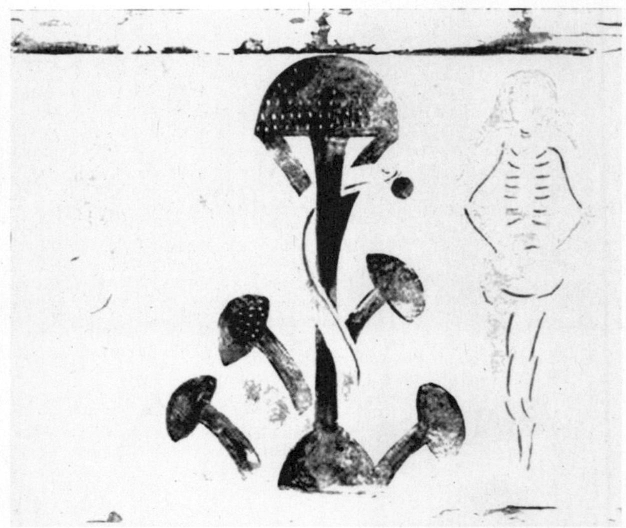
Fresco of Temptation in the Garden of Eden, Plaincourault Chapel, France, ca. 1299

In *The Sacred Mushroom* and the *Cross* published in 1970, British philologist John Marc Allegro presents his controversial thesis which postulates that early Christianity was a fertility cult based on the ingestion of hallucinogenic mushrooms and Jesus was merely a metaphor for the sacred mushroom. "[...] This is the basic origin of the stories of the New Testament. They were a literary device to spread the rites of mushroom worship to the faithful" — Allegro stated, receiving derision and discredit by the academic world. His theory was labelled as "a sensationalist lunatic theory" by *The Times* in 1971, reflecting the prevailing public opinion in England.

Source: R.Gordon Wasson, Soma

Shroomadelica

Shroomadelica is the term coined by music critic Marc Beaumont to indicate a short-lived music genre that combines funk and light psychedelia with and drug influenced—usually magic mushrooms—lyrics. The Shroomadelica scene was mainly active around the Liverpool area with bands as The Zutons and The Coral as main representative.

Credit: Deltasonic;
Source: Wikimedia Commons

Cover of the album *The Coral* by The Coral, 2002

Still Life with Insects and Amphibians

Dutch painter Otto Marseus van Schrieck, beloved among Cosimo III De Medici's court and the Amsterdam scientific community in the Dutch Golden Age, is the initiator of the "forest floor" still-life, a genre depicting the lowliest life of the forest ecosystem.

His paintings capture the intersection of art, science, and the occult by raising the Vermin, creatures so far associated with the Satanic powers, at subject of art. Indeed Van Schrieck is considered the first European artist to perceive and proclaim the aesthetic beauteous of mushrooms.

Many important painters like Leonardo already executed stunning studies of plants and animals, but van Schrieck was the first to sense the importance of the interdependence of plants, insects, mushrooms, and the wild creatures that lived in the undergrowth.

Otto Marseus van Schrieck's painting *Still Life with Insects and Amphibian*, 1614 ca.

Spore

Scan of electron microscope image of Agaricus bisporus' spores, 2007

As per the greek word spora "seed", in biology a spore describes a reproductive structure that is adapted for dispersion and capable of surviving for extended periods of time in unfavourable conditions. Fungal spores are microscopic biological particles serving a similar purpose to that of seeds in the plant world. Mushroom send an estimated fifty million tons of spores into the atmosphere each year worldwide.
Author: Dartmouth Electron Microscope Facility, Dartmouth College; Source: Wikimedia Commons

Telluride Mushroom Festival

Since 1981, the Telluride Mushroom Festival held annually in Telluride, Colorado, has been the first of this kind to offer an open forum for mushroom enthusiasts to discuss the latest in psychedelic, culinary, and medicinal mycology.
Source: Telluride.com

The Magic Mushrooms

The Magic Mushrooms was an American psychedelic garage rock band created in the 1960s by five students from the University of Pennsylvania in Philadelphia. Acclaimed Beat poet and countercultural thinker Allen Ginsberg suggested them the Magic Mushrooms's name after a campus lecture in late 1965.
Author: Ted Cahill;
Source: garagehangover.com

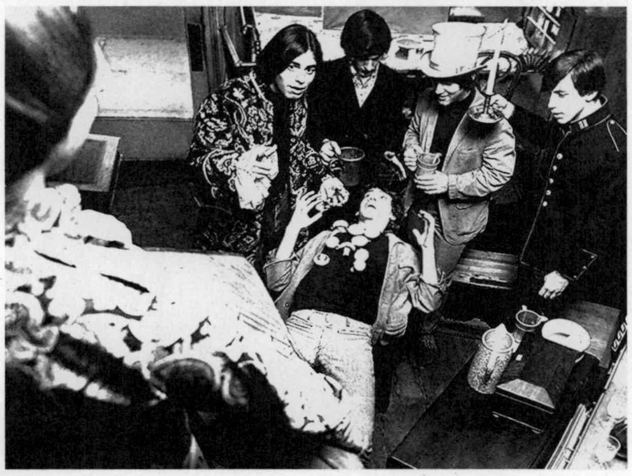

Photo promotion of the Magic Mushrooms band, Philadelphia, 1966

Photo promotion of the Magic Mushrooms band, Philadelphia, 1966

The Ocelli

The 2012 film *The Ocelli* (meaning "little eye") by Arka Group is an investigation in twenty-five parts on

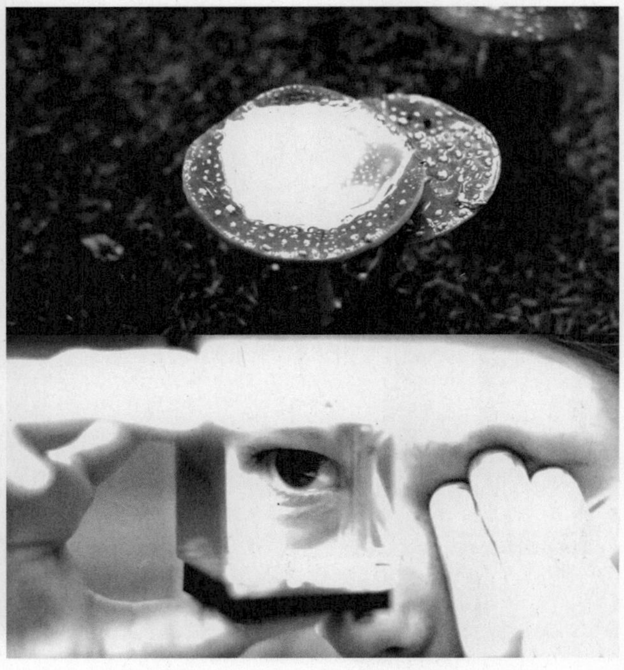

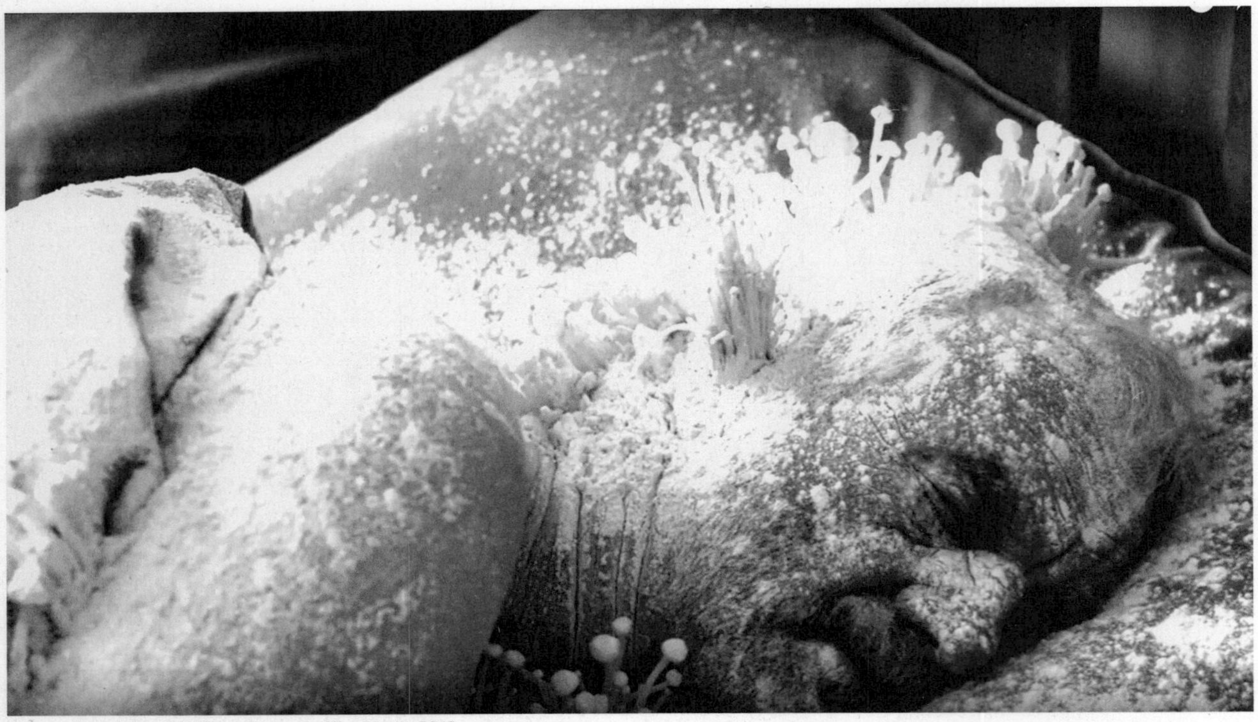

Screenshots from Arka Group's movie *The Ocelli*, 2012

Installation view of Anselm Kiefer's *Pour Madame de Stael: de l'Allemagne* at the Centre Pompidou in Paris, 2015

the perception and myth that charts the development of a 2,000 year-old mushroom from dormant state to sentient being. Through a poetic narrative that combines moving image, acted film, and unseen archival materials from the British Museum of Optometry, the film tells the story of a man who becomes infested by the spores of three-mile wide mushroom Armillaria which slowly consumes the body of the protagonist and thus becoming a conscious being.
Source: thearkagroup.org

The Shroom Project

Interdisciplinary artist Annie Ratti developed in 2013 The Shroom Project, a step-by-step installation on how to grow psychedelic mushrooms, following her physical and metaphysical fascination for the psilocybin mushroom. The installation consists of two Unités d'Habitation, named respectively Incubator and Growing Room designed and built for the mushrooms reproduction, and of a third element called Essicator, conceived to dry the mushrooms.

The Shroom Project is an investigation into the scientific, cultural and ethnographical significance of psilocybin mushrooms that enfolds the Western fascination with these rhizomatic organisms.
Photo: Leo van Kampen;
Credit: Annie Ratti;
Source: veeslehal.nl

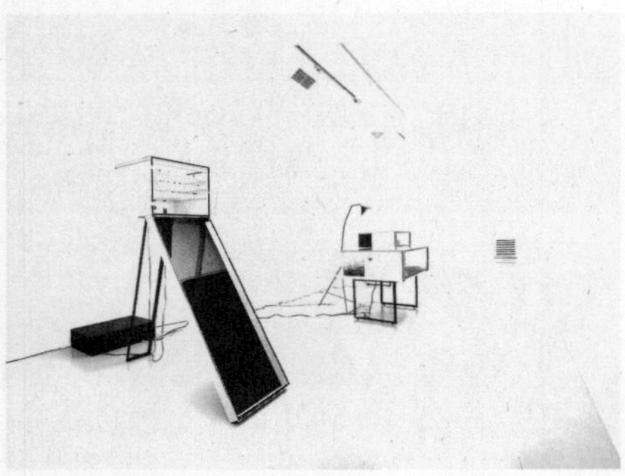

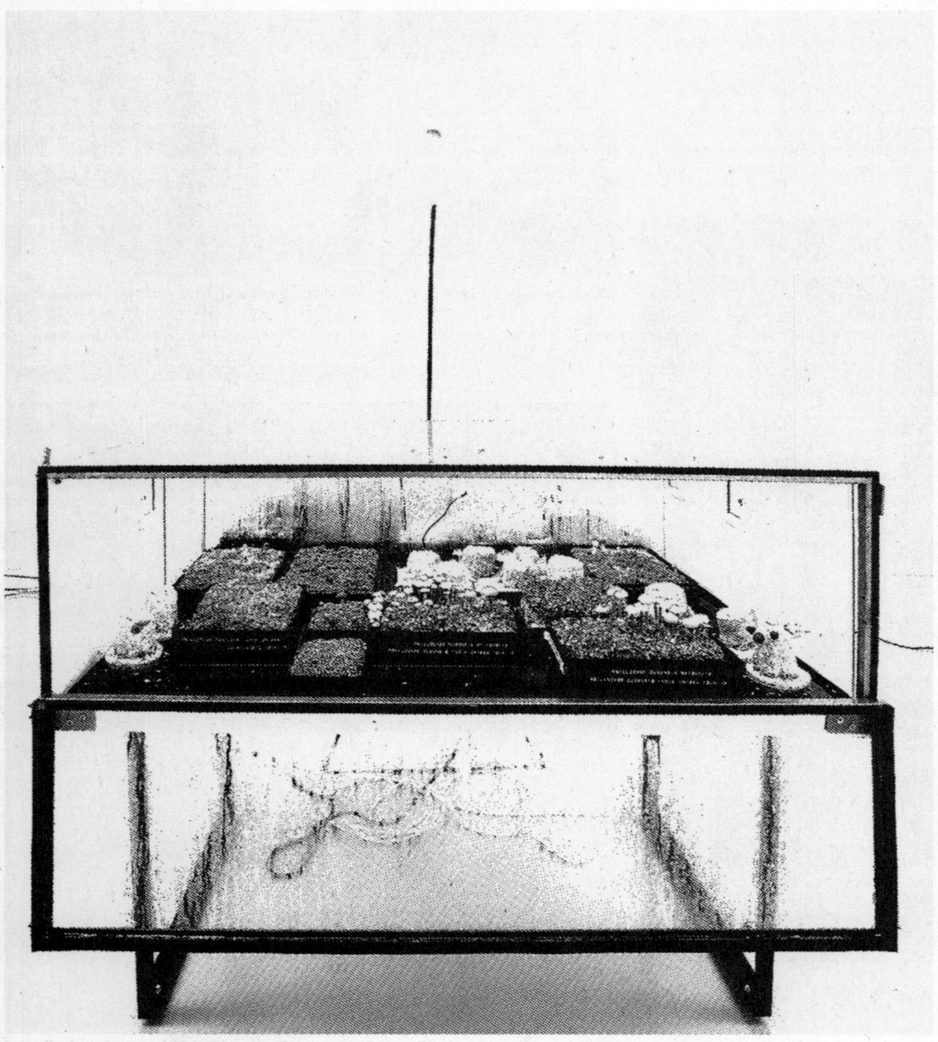

Installation views of *The Shroom Project* by Annie Ratti at Veeslehal, Middelburg, Netherlands, 2013

Theodore and the Talking Mushroom

Cover for the book *Theodore and the Talking Mushroom*, 1971

First published in 1971, this is a classic fable written and illustrated by four-time Caldecott Honor-winner Leo Lionni that tells the story of Theodore, a little mouse convinced to have no special talents. After the discovery of a blu mushroom that says "quirp" Theodore convinces his friends to have found the only talking mushroom in the world and that "quirp" means that he should be venerated above all animals. Theodore is bestowed with a crown until his friends learn that they've been deceived. Aside the beautiful collage illustrations, this tale provides a starting-point for discussions on honesty and the importance of being yourself.
Author: Leo Lionni;
Source: archive.org

Über l'Allemagne / Pour Madame de Staël: de l'Allemagne

Anselm Kiefer, among the most important artists of the post-war era, created for his retrospective Über Deutschland at the Pompidou Centre in Paris in 2015 the installation titled *Pour Madame de Stael: de l'Allemagne*. Giant mushrooms painted on cardboard spring from mountains of sand in front of a monumental painting of an eerie, magical forest. A military-style bed made for Red Army Faction (RAF) militant Ulrike Meinhof stands at the centre of the stage. The title is a direct reference to the French 19th century writer Madame de Staël and her 1810 book *De l'Allemagne*, considered the standard cultural history of the Goethe era.
Source: Welt.de

Victorian Fairy Paintings

Mushrooms began emerging into high art in 16th century during the reign of Queen Elizabeth I, but it is with the Victorian Era that toadstools find themselves to be prominent and common subjects of many British paintings. This genre is known as Fairy Painting and depict scenes of the hidden-from-view world of fairies and other subjects from the supernatural. Here mushrooms appear not just as outdoor decorations, but as part of the central theme.
Source: Wikimedia Commons

Voyage au Centre de la Terre

In 1864 Jules Verne's science fiction novel *Voyage au Centre de la Terre* there is a remarkable passage that tells about the encounter of the protagonists German professor Otto Lidenbrock and his nephew Axel with a forest of mushrooms of giant proportion.
"After we had gone about five hundred yards, we suddenly turned a steep promontory, and found ourselves close to a lofty forest! It consisted of straight trunks with tufted tops, in shape like parasols ... My uncle unhesitatingly called them by their real names. 'It is only,' he said, in his coolest manner, 'a forest of mushrooms.' ... I had heard that the Lycoperdon giganteum reaches nine feet in circumference, but here were white mushrooms, nearly forty feet high, and with tops of equal dimensions."
Author: Édouard Riou;
Source: Wikimedia Commons

Trading

"Buy low, sell high" is a classic trading strategy that has been found to apply not only for humans but to the Fungi Kingdom as well. The study recently published in Current Biology by evolutionary biologist Toby Kiers demonstrates that fungi are capable of sophisticated trading strategies, taking advantage of their plant-partners by shuttling goods to nutrient-starved areas where plants are willing to pay more than usual. Like canny merchants who know how to make a profit, fungi exploit resource scarcity by marking up their prices.
Source: quantamagazine.org

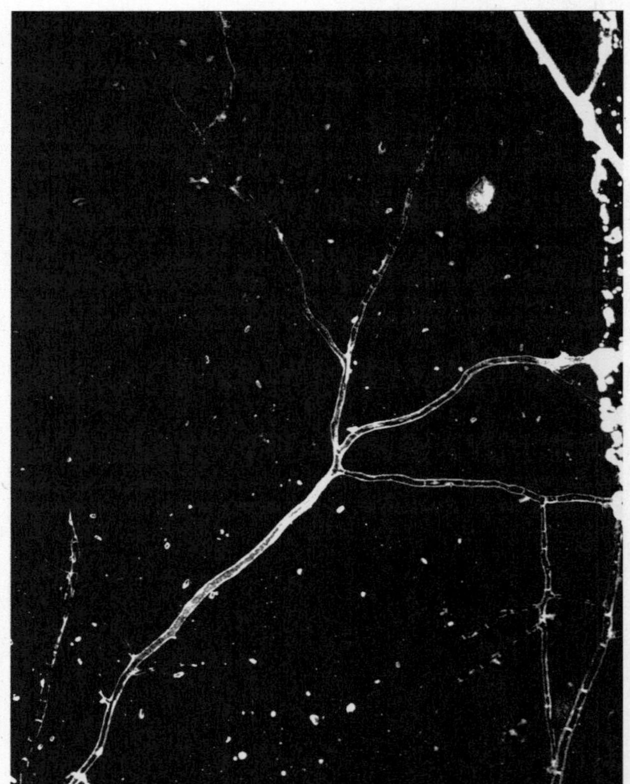

Micrograph of fungal hyphae depicting the streaming of nutrient biomolecules containing phosphorus

Photo of Richard Doyle's painting *Fairy Rings and Toadstools*, 1975

Both ethnomycologist R. Gordon Wasson and Doris Heyden, considered an authority on the religious symbolism of plants in precolumbian Mexico, believes that Xochipilli was most likely the patron deity of sacred hallucinogenic plants, in particular of the Amanita muscaria.

Source: mushroomstone.com

Xenolinguistics

The interest in the relationship between language, consciousness, and psychedelics is of longstanding. In 1973, scholar and writer Henry Munn noted in his book *The Mushrooms of Language how the influence of mushroom on language* was not unique to the Mazatecs Indians of Oaxaca, Mexico, but part of a shared reality by all experimenters of psilocybin substance.

Scholar Diana Reed Slattery coined the term Xenolinguistics to define the scientific study of languages of non-human intelligences, drawing on her eleven years' exploration to understand a symbolic language system, Glide, she acquired in an altered state of consciousness.

The findings of a recent study on the relationship between LSD and language by David Nutt, professor of neuropsychopharmacology at London's Imperial College, provide evidences as to why the effects of LSD on language allows quicker access to far way concepts stored in the mind and can result in the ability to help individuals notice or create new connections.

Source: mazerunner.wordpress.com

Illustration from Jules Verne's novel *Voyage au Centre de la Terre*, 1864

Miniature of the Aztec god Xochipilli now in the National Museum in Mexico City

Xochipilli

Xochipilli, whose name means "Prince of Flowers" in Nahuatl language, is the Aztec god of music, dance, flowers, and games. He is closely associated with Macuilxochitl, or Five Flowers.

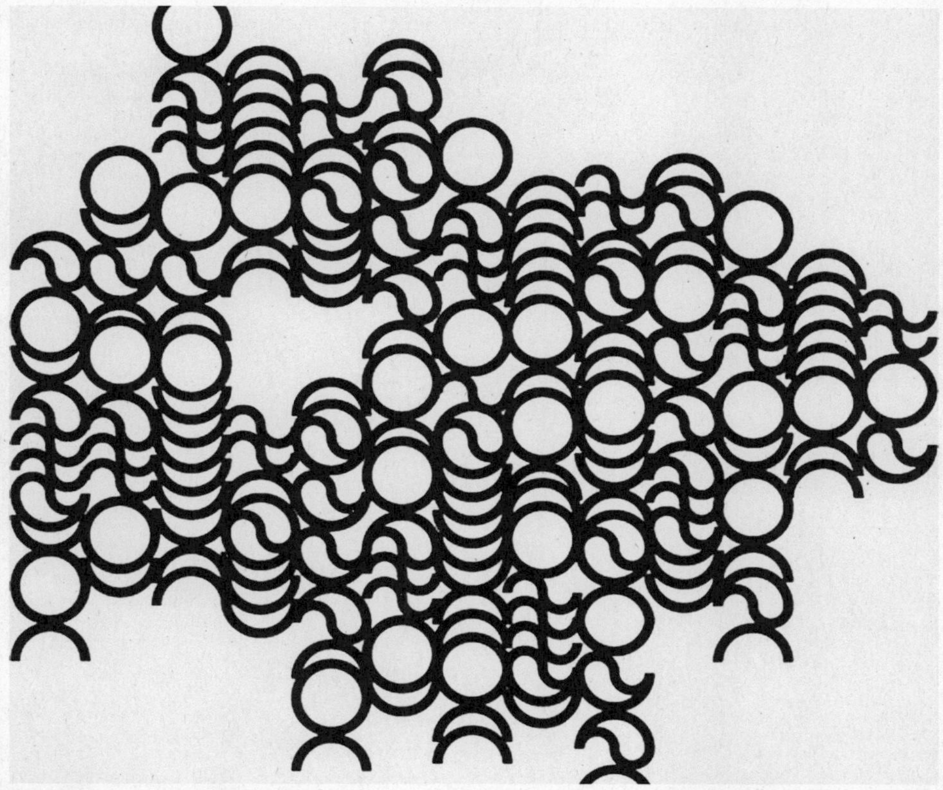

Glide Maze, a combination of glyphs from the symbolic language system called Glide acquired by Diana Slattery

White Rabbit

White Rabbit is a song written by singer Grace Slick and recorded with San Fransisco psychedelic rock band Jefferson Airplane in the 1967 album *Surrealistic Pillow*. It became immediately a hit peaking at #8 on Billboard Hot 100 and in 2004 *Rolling Stone* included the song in the list of 500 Greatest Songs of All Time.

The song-title is a direct reference to the imagery from the *Alice In Wonderland* novel, as Slick identifies herself as Alice escaping the rigid 1950s American society reserved to women, while the lyrics illustrate the sensory distortions experience with hallucinogenic drugs.

White Rabbit ended up eventually on "blacklists"' at several radio stations after being banned by the Illinois Crime Commission as one of the "drug-oriented rock records" that would feed a LSD and more general psychedelics-based culture.

Author: RCA Records;
Source: Billboard

Trade ad for Jefferson Airplane *White Rabbit* single, 17 June 1967

Wood Wide Web

The Wood Wide Web is the colloquial nickname for the mychorrizal networks, defined in a 2008 TED Talk by mycologist Paul Stamets as the "Earth's natural internet" by analogy to the many roles intermediated by the World Wide Web. Back to the 1970s, Stamets had already noticed strong similarities between mycelia and ARPANET, the US Department of Defense's early version of the internet. The fungal internet exemplifies one of the great lessons of ecology: seemingly separate organisms are often connected and they depend on each other.

Source: wrongplanet.net

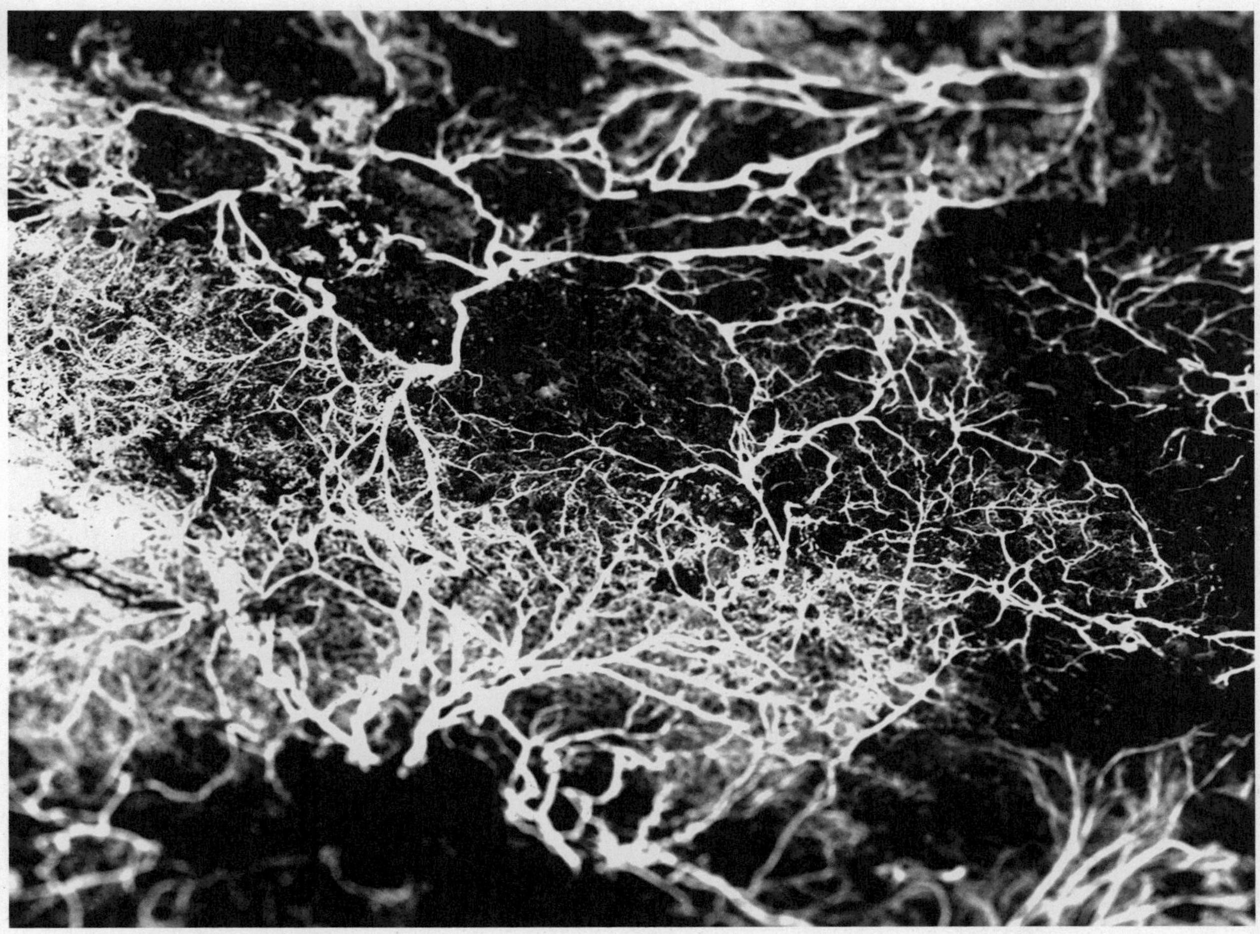

Detail of the mycorrhizal fungi-network.

We decided to build a big dome before we the land
we were to build it on. We bought lumber at the lumber
mill and shingles at the shingle store.
money and more sense we think of building our sleeping
shelters out WHAT IS HERE. One
out of stone planned here) others made
from adobe bricks, etc.
moulding gleaned from old buildings.
Glass in these parts
owners who are currently replacing all
with corrugated fiberglass.
Even here where it is plentiful it's
12 cents a board unseasoned stuff. Used
have just finished building
a garage/shop. The and roof are all built
with free second hand the lumber that we did
buy for the building low grade but made
fine siding because grooved it ourselves.
(Simply a matter of inexpensive moulding head
attachment for our fancy sliding garage
doors, which we bought for $20
from a garage in modernizing.
We have learned money and more scavenging
we are building structures.
true in food,
care,

Further Readings

Lukas Feireiss, Leopold Banchini

An eclectic collection of manual-like publications, that serve as a basic introduction to countercultural models of living. Beyond the realm of conventional thinking, these unique sourcebooks offer alternative perspectives on a wide array of topics such as Shelter, Survival, Community, Design, Environment, Education, Revolution, Spirituality, and Psychedelics. These topical categories distinguish the selected publications from one another, but are principally open and, even more so, invite for reciprocal exchange.

Shelter

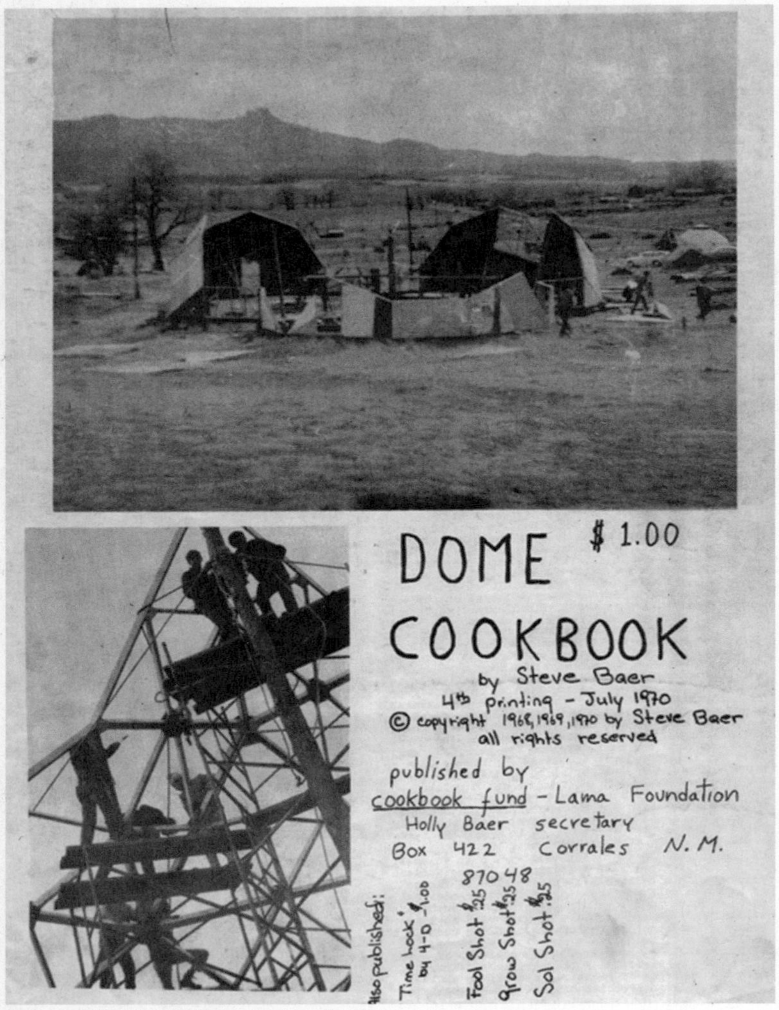

Cover for Steve Baer's *Dome Cookbook*, 1968

Dome Cookbook

Steve Baer, 1968

Dome Cookbook is an early newsprint zine dedicated to the building of geodesic domes. It was created in 1968 by Steve Baer, beatnik engineer and resident of Drop City, an intentional community in southern Colorado established in 1965 and considered as the first rural hippie commune.

Credit: Lama Foundation.
Source: MoMA.org

Inflatocookbook

Ant Farm, 1971

Inflatocookbook is an illustrated guide to the art of building one's own inflatable structure first published in 1971 by Ant Farm, a multidisciplinary collective established within the counter-cultural milieu of 1968 San Francisco. In contrast with the Brutalist movement, the Inflatable architecture fitted Ant Farm's ideals for fluidity, freedom of movement, and communal lifestyles.

Cover and scans Ant Farm's *Inflatocookbook*, 1971.

Cover for Ken Isaacs' *How to Build Your Own Living Structure*, 1974

Cover for Ken Isaacs' *How to Build Your Own Living Structure*, 1974

How to Build Your Own Living Structure

Ken Isaacs, 1974

American architectural experimenter Ken Isaacs wrote his *How to Build Your Own Living Structure* in 1974 and even today it is regarded as a classic of utopian architecture.
This manual contains Isaacs' guidelines to make a variety of flexible experimental indoor interiors, storage units, and a micro-house according to his concept of a matrix-based modular system to configure the volume of a room into and multi-functional living structures.

Domebook

Lloyd Kahn, 1970

Lloyd Kahn, editor-in-chief of Shelter Publications and pioneer of the green building and green architecture movements, published in 1970 his first book *Domebook One*, followed the next year with *Domebook 2*, which sold more than 165,000 copies.
Inspired by the geodesic design principles of Buckminster Fuller, this book is considered the countercultural bible of dome-building and a source of inspiration for the back-to-land-movement. However, after living in his dome for a year, Kahn concluded that domes did not work well and as consequently stopped the printing of *Domebook 2*.

Domebook One. Source: shelterpress.org; Domebook 2.
Source: Amazon

Cover for Lloyd Kahn's *Domebook One*, 1970

Cover for Lloyd Kahn's *Domebook 2*, 1971

Cover for the 40th anniversary edition of Llyod Kahn's *Shelter*

Shelter

Lloyd Kahn, and Bob Easton, 1973

First published in 1973, *Shelter* publication by Lloyd Kahn and Bob Easton is a classic, celebrating the past and present of organic architecture. Drawing on the spirit of the 1960s' counterculture, this compendium narrates the history of shelter and the evolution of building types, complemented by a rich section on building materials that demonstrates resourcefulness and exuberance of human habitat.
In 1978, it followed *Shelter 2*, a practical book for an owner-builder interested in constructing a simple stud-frame house.

Source: Llyod's blog

Survival

Cover of one of the revisited editions of *Donde No Hay Doctor handbook*, 1970

Donde No Hay Doctor

David Werner, 1970

Donde No Hay Doctor [Where There Is No Doctor: A Village Health Care Handbook], originally written in 1970 by biologist and public health worker David Werner during is experiences at his Project Piaxtla in in Ajoya, Mexico, it is considered by the World Health Organization to be the most widely-used health-care manual in the world with over one hundred translations and millions copies sold. This practical guide covers a wide range of health aspects, from common diseases to nutrition to postnatal care, and places special emphasis on prevention as the primary way to recognise and treat many common sicknesses.

Dwelling Portably

Bert Davis, and Holly Davis, 1980–2012

This monthly zine, formerly called Message Post, was published as of 1980 for several decades by Holly and Bert Davis, who lived a nomad life for 30 years. *Dwelling Portably* provides guidance for those who have chosen to live without a permanent residence or low-budget in-motion life in the US. How to live in cars, how to buy staples for 25 cents per pound, where to find a cheap dentist, or the dangers of social services taking kids without a house are just some of the many practical advices available in this book.

Source: Amazon

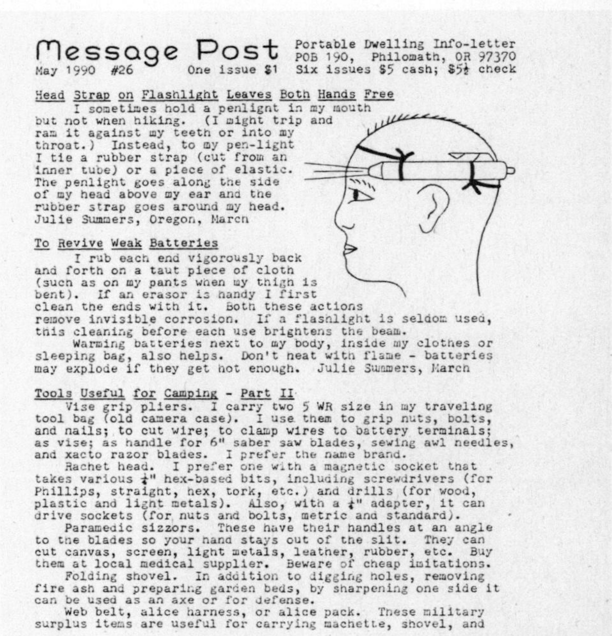

Message Post
May 1990 #26 One issue $1
Portable Dwelling Info-letter
POB 190, Philomath, OR 97370
Six issues $5 cash; $5½ check

Head Strap on Flashlight Leaves Both Hands Free

I sometimes hold a penlight in my mouth but not when hiking. (I might trip and ram it against my teeth or into my throat.) Instead, to my pen-light I tie a rubber strap (cut from an inner tube) or a piece of elastic. The penlight goes along the side of my head above my ear and the rubber strap goes around my head. Julie Summers, Oregon, March

To Revive Weak Batteries

I rub each end vigorously back and forth on a taut piece of cloth (such as on my pants when my thigh is bent). If an erasor is handy I first clean the ends with it. Both these actions remove invisible corrosion. If a flashlight is seldom used, this cleaning before each use brightens the beam.

Warming batteries next to my body, inside my clothes or sleeping bag, also helps. Don't heat with flame - batteries may explode if they get hot enough. Julie Summers, March

Tools Useful for Camping - Part II

Vise grip pliers. I carry two 5 WR size in my traveling tool bag (old camera case). I use them to grip nuts, bolts, and nails; to cut wire; to clamp wires to battery terminals; as vise; as handle for 6" saber saw blades, sewing awl needles, and xacto razor blades. I prefer the name brand.

Rachet head. I prefer one with a magnetic socket that takes various ¼" hex-based bits, including screwdrivers (for Phillips, straight, hex, tork, etc.) and drills (for wood, plastic and light metals). Also, with a ¼" adapter, it can drive sockets (for nuts and bolts, metric and standard).

Paramedic sizzors. These have their handles at an angle to the blades so your hand stays out of the slit. They can cut canvas, screen, light metals, leather, rubber, etc. Buy them at local medical supplier. Beware of cheap imitations.

Folding shovel. In addition to digging holes, removing fire ash and preparing garden beds, by sharpening one side it can be used as an axe or for defense.

Web belt, alice harness, or alice pack. These military surplus items are useful for carrying machette, shovel, and

Extract from *Dwelling Portably* Info-letter No.26 by Bert and Holly Davis, May 1990

Last reprint of the *US Army Survival Manual* originally printed in 1957

Whole Earth Catalog

Stewart Brand, 1968

Stewart Brand was at the heart of the counterculture movement when in 1968 he published the first edition of the *Whole Earth Catalog*, set to become the magnum opus of the entire counterculture scene of the late 1960s and later acknowledged as the conceptual forerunner of the Internet.

Defined as how-to manual, compendium, encyclopedia, literary review, opinionated life guide, collection of readers' recommendations and reviews, the Catalog served essentially as paper-database to democratise the access to any kind of information ranging from bookmaking to dolphin communication, from computational physics to goat husbandry, providing the tools to apply individual initiative to shape an alternative—more conscious—future.

As John Markoff, a technology writer for the *New York Times*, puts it, the *Whole Earth Catalog* was "the internet before the internet. It was the book of the future. It was a web in newsprint."

Stewart Brand's *Whole Earth Catalog*, 1968. Source: e-flux

US Army Survival Manual: FM 21-76

Department of Defence, 1957

The *US Army Survival Manual* printed by the US Department of Defence in 1957, it is still in use as the source that provides step-by-step instructions for all extreme circumstances. Based entirely on the keyword "survival," the FM 21-76 was first developed to train soldiers to survive in hostile and unfamiliar territory. As such this manual will teach you how to build makeshift shelters, procure food and water, cook a meal, identify edible and poisonous plants, avoid dangerous animals, treat wounds and illness, navigate with the sun and stars, make weapons and equipment, and much more.

Source: the US Department of Defence.

First cover and layout for Stewart Brand's *Whole Earth Catalog*, 1968

Community

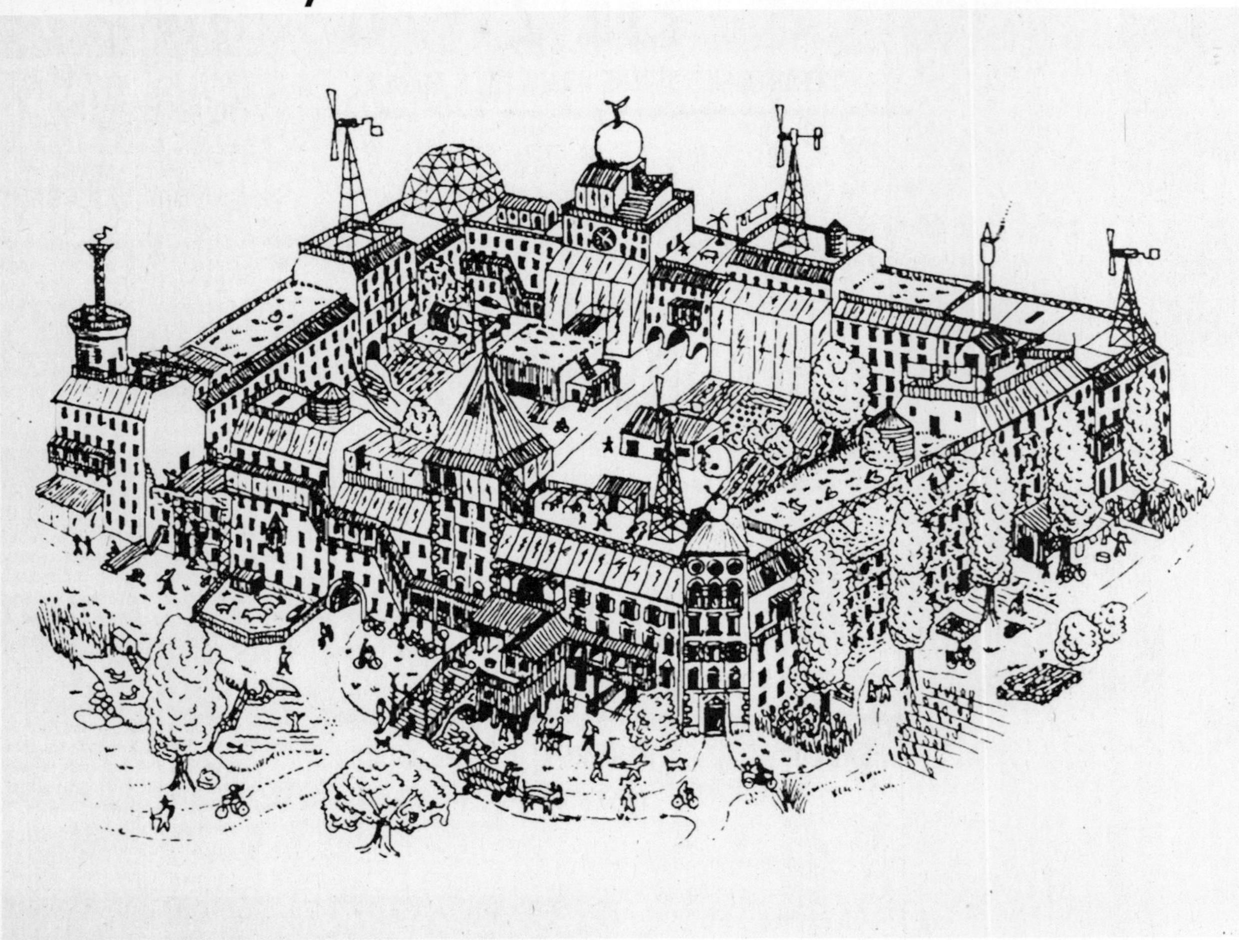

Illustration for an urban bolo model as conceived by p.m., 1984.

Cover for Leslie Clark Stevens' est: The Steersman Handbook, Charts of the Coming Decade of Conflict, 1970

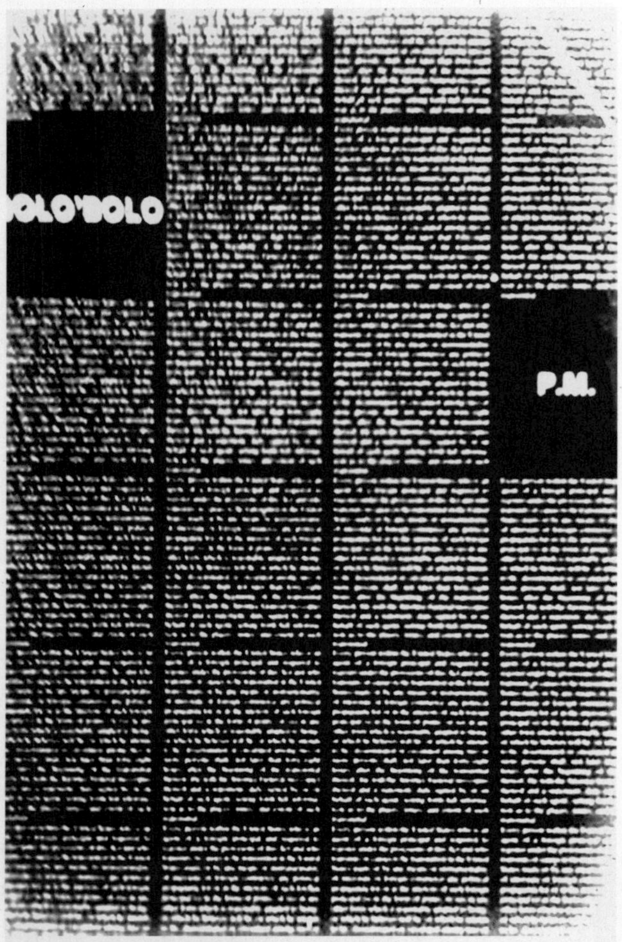

Cover for the first edition of *bolo'bolo* by p.m., 1984

bolo' bolo

p.m., 1984

Published in 1984, *bolo'bolo* by p.m., the pseudonym for Swiss author Hans Widmer is considered one of the most significant social utopian texts of the late 20th century.

The title of the book refers to the bolo, a self-sufficient community that constitutes the basic social unit in an envisioned sustainable, ecological future.

Bolo'bolo can be read as a plan for transformation from capitalism to another system based on local organization and a microclimate of cultures that form the unit of social cohesion.

Cover of *bolo'bolo*;
Source: goodreads.com;
Illustration;
Source: Wikimedia Commons

Drop City

Peter Rabbit, 1971

The 1971 little publication *Drop City* by Peter Rabbit, author and Drop City resident, narrates the story and the value of the inhabitants of the community. Drop City was an intentional community in southern Colorado established in 1965 and abandoned in 1973. Despite the fact that did not last long, Drop City attracted international attention and inspired a generation of counterculture communities. The Drop City crew was inspired by the geodesic design principles of Buckminster Fuller when they started to hand-build their geodesic domes out of "the garbage of America" and this is recalled as the first time geodesic domes were used for domestic living.

Source: Amazon

Cover of Peter Rabbit's *Drop City*, 1971

est: The Steersman Handbook

Leslie Clark Stevens, 1970

est: The Steersman Handbook, Charts of the Coming Decade of Conflict is a work of science-fiction cast as a nonfictional study that describes a future society made by a new generation of postliterate humans with the qualities necessary for social transformation integral to Earth's survival, the "est people". Though the book was speculative in nature, Leslie Steven's work and the concept behind "est", acronym for "Electronic Social Transformation", has been referenced in later sociological evaluations of potential paths for society.

Source: Amazon

Design

Da Cosa Nasce Cosa

Bruno Munari, 1981

Written by Bruno Munari, one of the most celebrated names of the 20th century Italian panorama of visual arts, *Da Cosa Nasce Cosa* tells the basic rules of good design with dozens of photos, diagrams, drawings and projects that demonstrates how to design is not the innate talent of the few. In Munari's words: "The design method is nothing more than a series of operations necessary, arranged in a logical order dictated by experience. Its purpose is to achieve maximum results with minimum effort".
Source: Anobii

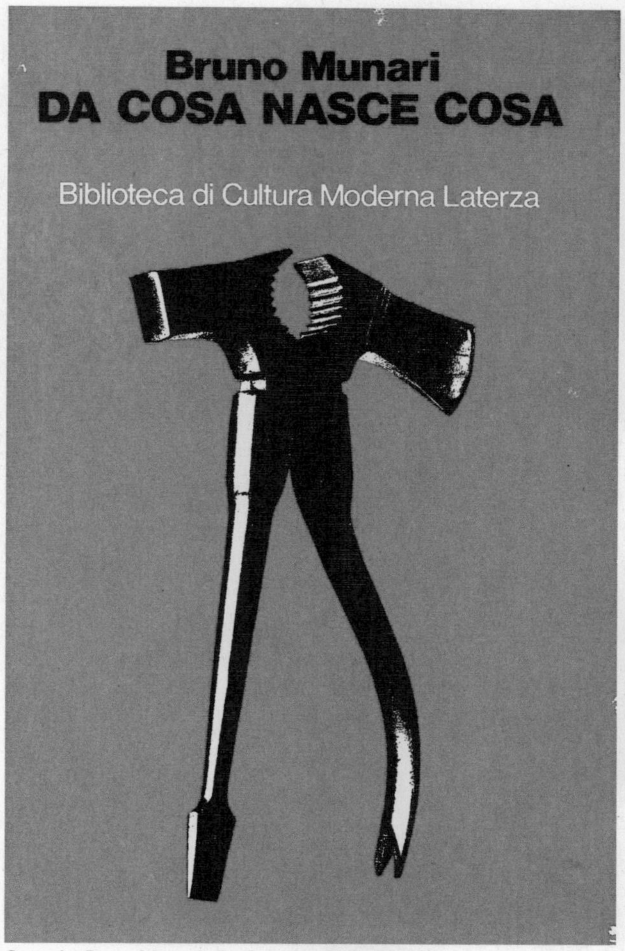

Cover for Bruno Munari's *Da Cosa Nasce Cosa*, 1981

Auto-progettazione?

Enzo Mari, 1974

In 1974, Italian designer Enzo Mari published the first edition of *Autoprogettazione?*, a manual which includes a number of furniture projects that could be realized potentially by anyone through wooden boards and simple tools. According to Enzo Mari's vision, these projects do not want to be alternatives to industrial production but rather exercises which may help each one understand how industrial products work and help to develop a critical eye towards them.
Source: Corraini Edizioni

Nomadic Furniture

Victor Papanek and James Hennessey, 1973

With *Nomadic Furniture 1*, published in 1973 and followed-up by *Nomadic Forniture 2*, designers Victor Papanek and James Hennessey set out to change the world by empowering people to create their own inexpensive furnishings. Nomadic Furniture publications contain diagrams of DIY plans and simple instructions for cardboard seats, bookshelves, lamps made from milk jugs, hexagonal dining sets, in line with the subtitle that reads "how to build and where to buy lightweight furniture that folds, inflates, knocks down, stacks, or is disposable and can be recycled."
Source: Core 77

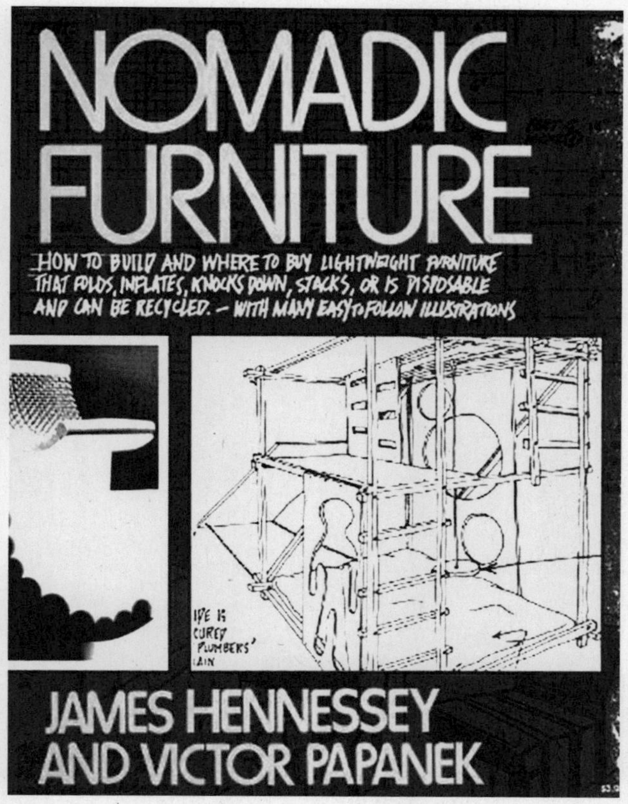

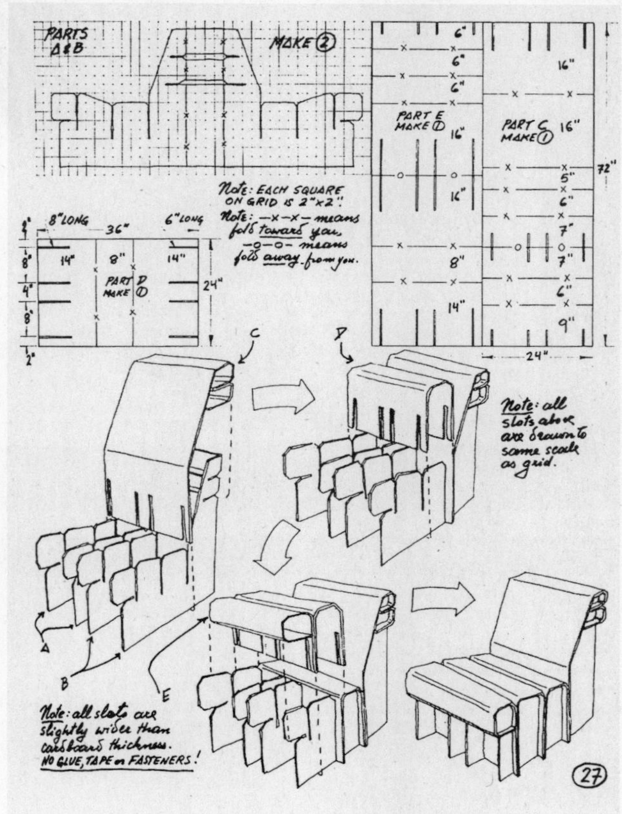

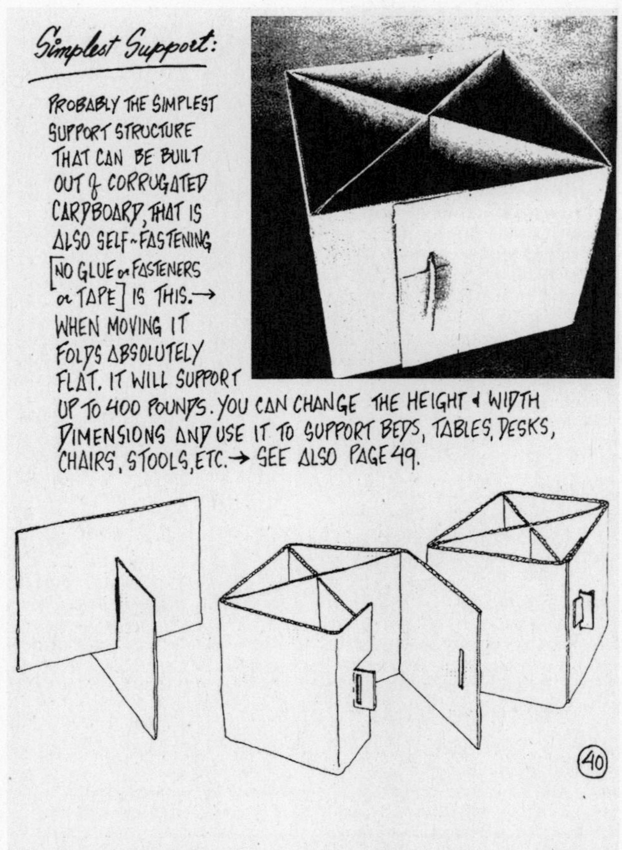

Cover for the first edition of *Nomadic Furniture* and images of step-by-step instructions included in the book written by Victor Papanek, and James Hennessey, 1973

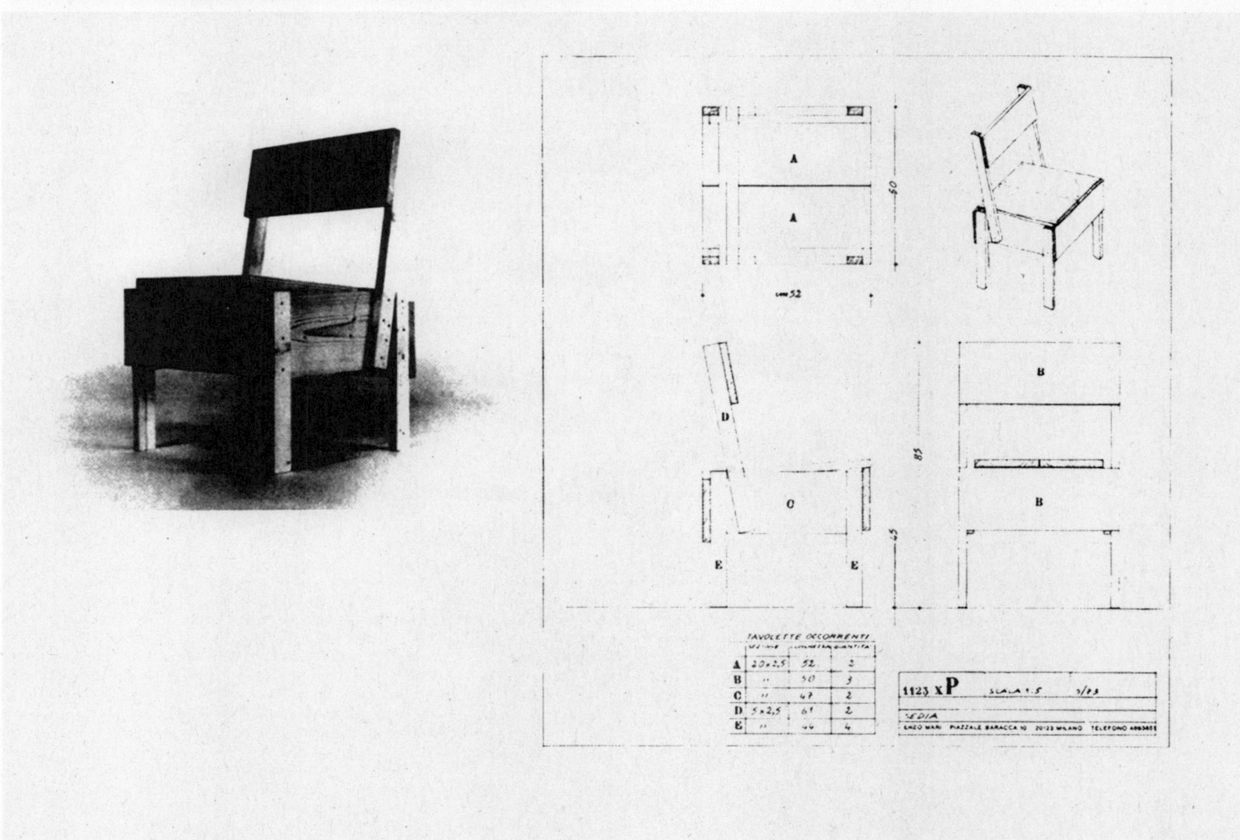

Cover and spread for Enzo Mari's *Autoprogettazione?*, 1974.

Environment

Cover for the issue No.6 and No.38 of CoEvolution Quarterly published by Stewart Brand

CoEvolution Quarterly

Stewart Brand, 1974–1984

In 1974, the *Whole Earth Catalog's* father Stewart Brand published *Co-Evolution Quarterly*, a journal focussed on environmentalism. Build upon the *Whole Earth Catalog*, the forty-three issues published until fall of 1984 tackled questions spanning from science to sociology, from the arts to politics and technology.
CQ's statement of purpose read in part "We are dedicated to demystification, to self-teaching, and to encouraging people to think for themselves. Thus, our Motto: 'access to tools and ideas' ... We recommend rather than attack ... We change with the times that we help change ... We update ourselves continually ... We're not a 'political' magazine ... We are deliberately eclectic."
Source: Amazon

Operating Manual for Spaceship Earth

Richard Buckminster Fuller, 1969

How will humanity survive? How does automation influence individualization? How can we utilize our resources more effectively to realize our potential to end poverty in this generation? asks theorist, designer and futurist Buckminster Fuller in his 1969 popular short book Operating Manual for Spaceship Earth. Fuller's book is a call for a dramatic shift in our attitude towards our "Spaceship Earth" and envisages a prosperous human future based on care for and respect for Earth finite number of resources.
Source: Vintage Books

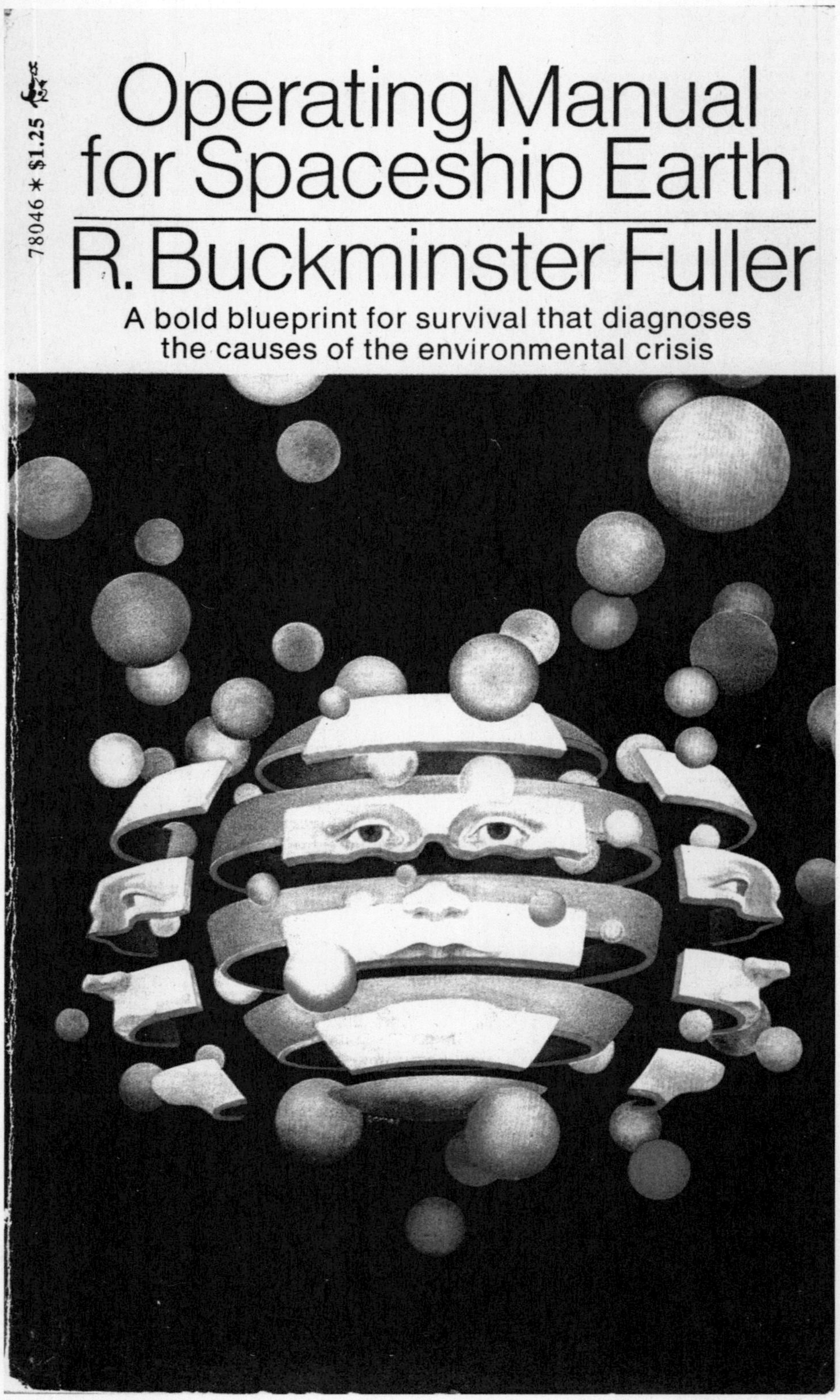

Front cover of one of the first editions of R. Buckminster Fuller's *Operating Manual for Spaceship Earth*, 1969

Education

Manual for Civilization

The Long Now Foundation, 1996

“What books would you want to restart civilization from scratch?” is the foundational question for the creation of the Manual for Civilization, a crowdsourced library of roughly 3,500 books started by The Long Now Foundation’s Executive Director Alexander Rose in 1996 to create a record—and democratize—the most essential human knowledge. From Denis Diderot’s famous Encyclopedie to Stewart Brand’s countercultural bible *Whole Earth Catalog*, Manual for Civilization counts already 1,000 titles collected by The Foundation through submissions from over 6,000 members and experts, including Brian Eno, Stewart Brand, Kevin Kelly, Maria Popova, and Violet Blue, and can be found at The Interval, in San Francisco.
Source: brainpickings.org

Photo of part of the Manual for Civilisation’s library initiated by The Long Now Foundation

Global Tools

Global Tools, 1973-1975

Global Tools is a three years’ alternative pedagogy for design that took place between Florence, Milan and Naples in the early 1970s. The Radical Florentine groups around Global Tools took inspiration from other experiments around the world like the *Whole Earth Catalog*—significantly subtitled Access to Tools—to take a critical stance against laissez-faire capitalism and overproduction in design. Global Tools framed a counter-school of design that would reinvest value in collective and non-expert design practice to abolish the division of manual work and intellectual creativity, hierarchies and competition.
Source: MAXXI

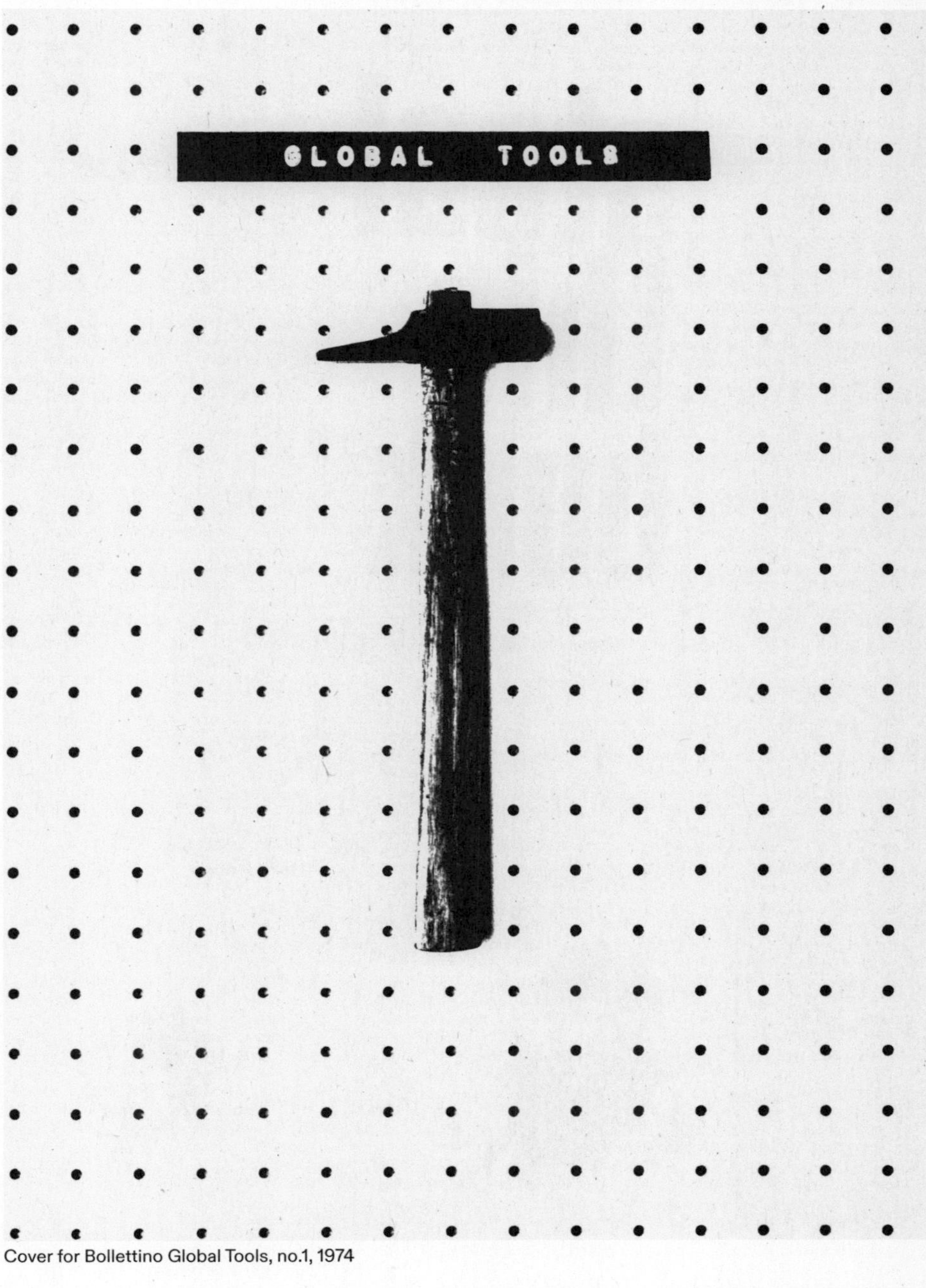

Cover for Bollettino Global Tools, no.1, 1974

Cover for the 1970 edition of Teaching as a Subversive Activity, by Neil Postman and Charles Weingartner, 1969

Teaching as a Subversive Activity

Neil Postman and Charles Weingartner, 1969

First published in 1969, *Teaching as a Subversive Activity* by co-authors Neil Postman and Charles Weingartner, has been outlined as one of the most radical book in the history of education. The book challenges the dominant American education system of the time by proposing an innovative education setting based on the concept of student-centered learning, that encourage students to learn by asking questions instead of by teachers giving lectures.

Teach Your Own

John Holt, 1981

In 1981, pioneer of the youth right movement, author and educator John Holt wrote *Teach your Own* and introduced his “homeschooling” methodology for the first time.
In John Holt words “This book is about ways we can teach children, or rather, allow them to learn, outside of schools at home, or in whatever other places and situations (and the more the better) we can make available to them.”
Teach Your Own is considered a classic text for the growing new generation of homeschooling parents.
Source: Amazon

Cover of the first edition of John Holt’s *Teach Your Own*, 1981

Revolution

Cover for Jerry Rubin's Do It!, 1970

Do It!

Jerry Rubin, 1970

Do It! Scenarios of the Revolution written in 1970 by American political activist and icon of the anti-war movement Jerry Rubin, it has been described as as the "Communist Manifesto" of the era. The book is a series of forty-three vignettes that call for revolutionary change against capitalism in the US in the theatre of everyday life rather than through abstract theorising.
Source: Abebook

Oz

Richard Neville,
1967 – 1973

Oz, the controversial underground magazine, is a major record of the counterculture revolution of the 1960s. While it was first published in Sydney in 1963, a parallel version was released in London from 1967 with Richard Neville as central editor in both countries. During the run of 48 issues, Oz tackled subjects ranging from gay rights to racism, environment, feminism, sex, acid, rock music and the Vietnam War, becoming the enfant terrible of the underground press.
Source: Wikimedia Commons

Steal this book

Abbie Hoffman, 1971

Meant as a practical guide for the aspiring hippies, *Steal This Book* by American political and social activist Abbie Hoffman is considered as the countercultural tract par excellence. At first rejected by at least thirty publishers, this manual for survival in the America of the 1960s became a cult classic with over 250,000 copies sold during the first months from its publication in 1971. Hoffman's book is divided into three sections, "Survive!", "Fight!", and "Liberate!", each one of them filled with advices on ways to fight the government and corporations in any way possible.
Source: pbagalleries.com

First edition of *Steal this Book* signed by its author Abbie Hoffman, 1971

Spirituality

Cover for Carlos Castaneda's *A Separate Reality: Further Conversations with Don Juan*, 1971

A Separate Reality

Carlos Castaneda, 1971

Published in 1971, *A Separate Reality: Further Conversations with Don Juan* is the second book of the trilogy written by anthropologist and author Carlos Castaneda concerning the events that took place during his apprenticeship with a Yaqui Indian Shaman, Don Juan Matus.
The book contains an introduction, an epilogue and two separate parts that describe Matus' attempts to get the author learn how to "see", meaning the process of "perceiving energy directly as it flows through the universe".

Le Matin des Magiciens

Louis Pauwels and Jacques Bergier, 1960

The groundbreaking Le Matin du Magiciens (The Morning of the Magicians]) written by journalists Louis Pauwels and Jacques Bergier and first published in 1960, is an international bestseller and conspiracy-theory enthusiasts' favourite book. The book challenges the common perception of reality by supporting the existence of paranormal activity, telepathy, and extraterrestrial communications aside from covering a wide range of topics like cryptohistory, occultism in Nazism, alchemy and spiritual philosophy.
Source: Antiqbook

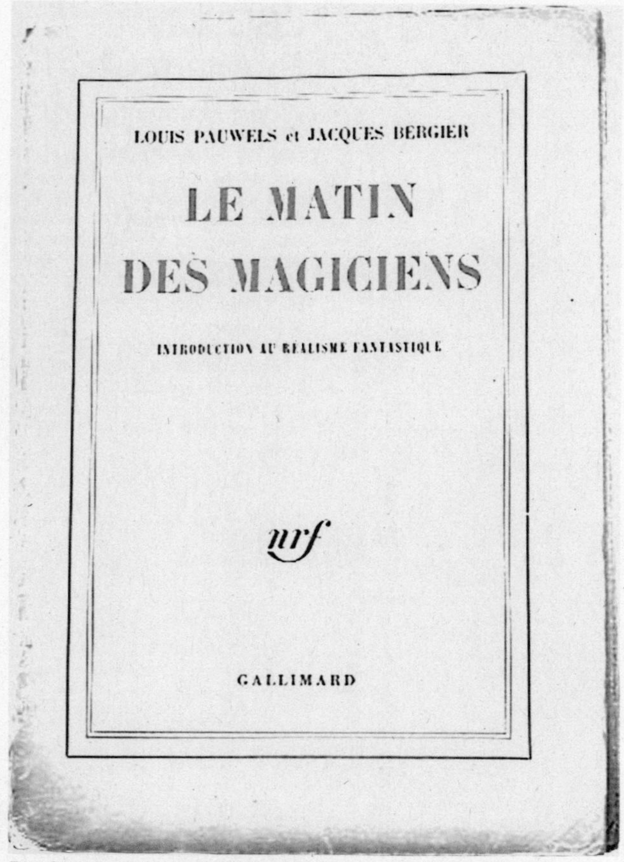

First front cover for *Le Matin des Magicians* by Louis Pauwels and Jacques Bergier, 1961

The San Francisco Oracle

Allen Cohen and Michael Bowen, 1966 – 1968

The San Francisco Oracle, with poet Allen Cohen and artist Michael Bowen at the helm as editor and art director, was an underground newspaper known for weaving spirituality, poetry and progressive ideas with psychedelic imagery in the late 1960s.
The publication was only distributed for about two years (from September 1966 to January 1968), but it became well-known around the world for its countercultural vision and unique form during the social and political movements of the time.
In Cohen's words, it was meant to serve as "a guide for young people who wanted to step outside the realms of the type of conventional thinking that was so prevalent in their parents' and earlier generations".
Source: Wikiwand

Ashtanga Yoga Primer

Baba Hari Dass, 1977

Yoga Master Baba Hari Dass published in 1977 an easy to use manual of the traditional practices of Ashtanga Yoga, which is the path of internal purification for revealing the Universal Self outlined by the sage Patanjali in the Yoga Sutras. The manual includes beginning and intermediate practices for purification, breath control, meditation, mudras, and yoga postures, along with basic theory of yoga metaphysics, daily practice schedules, and a Sanskrit glossary.
Source: Amazon

Cover for *Ashtanga Yoga Primer* by Baba Hari Dass, 1977. Further Conversations with Don Juan, *1971*

Cover Vol.1 No.5 for the *San Francisco Oracle* publication, January 1967

Psychedelics

LSD, My Problem Child

Albert Hofmann, 1979

LSD, My Problem Child is the inside story of LSD told by his father, the organic chemist Albert Hofmann. The book traces the path of one of the most important scientific discoveries of our time from a promising psychiatric research medicine to a recreational drug sparking hysteria and prohibition.

First front cover for the German edition of Albert Hofmann's LSD, My Problem Child, 1979. Source: Amazon

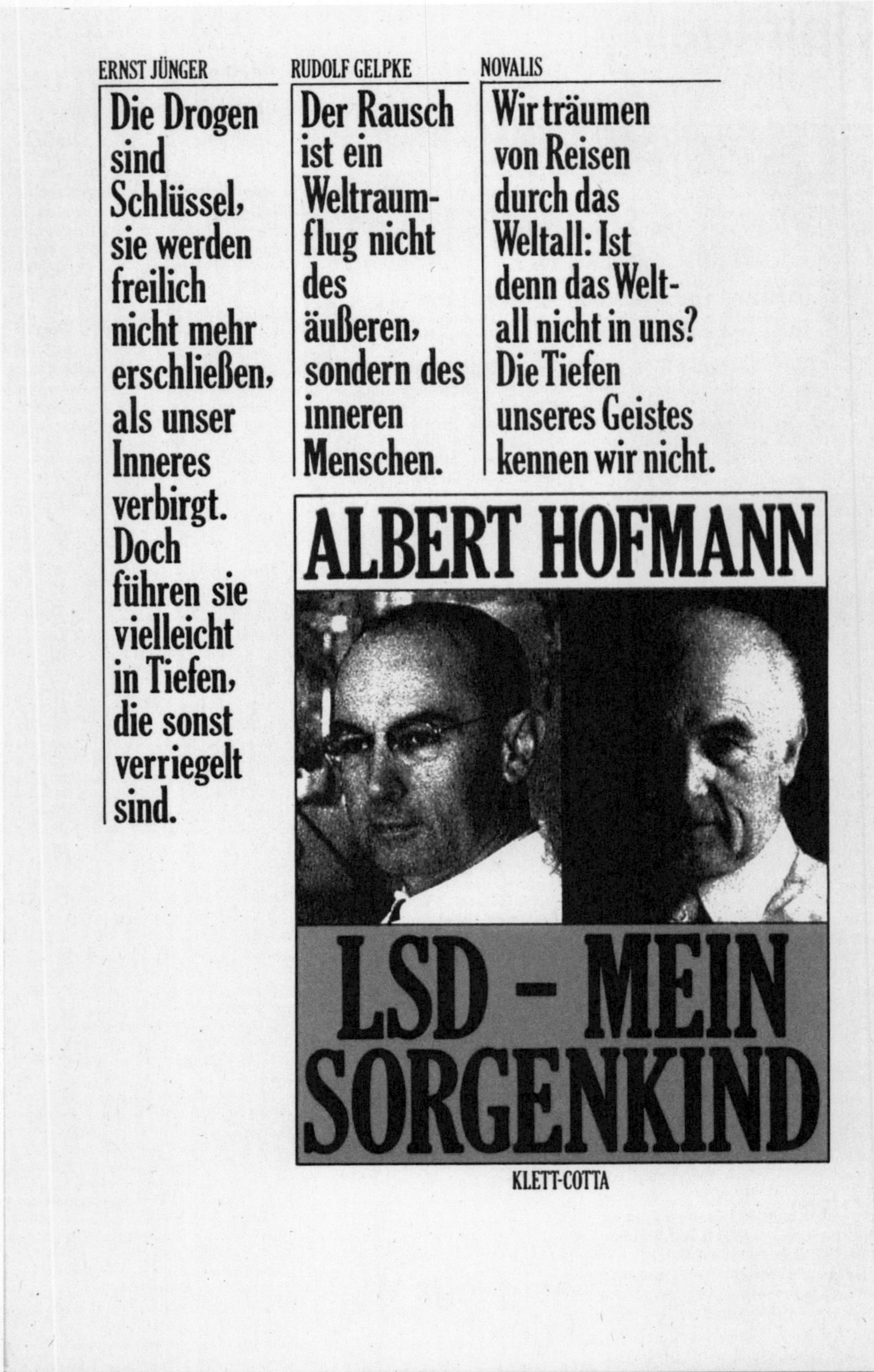

Inner Space. The Magazine of the Psychedelic Community

1966

The October 1966 first issue of *Inner Space* zine was born as a reaction to the offensive gave to the use of psychedelic substances in the America of the late 1960s.
Subtitled "The Magazine of the Psychedelic Community," this early zine presented itself as a "clearing-house for information, and as a forum for the discussion of the use of psychedelics" and included articles by important writers and psychologists advocating the potential of hallucinogenic drugs, such as Timothy Leary, Lisa Bieberman, Art Kleps, and Peter Stafford, author of the Psychedelics Encyclopedia.
Source: beat books.com

Cover of *Inner Space's* second issue "A Gentle Guide Through the Current Hysteria...", Dec. 1966

The Psychedelic Experience

Timothy Leary, Ralph Metzner and Richard Alpert, 1964

The Psychedelic Experience: A Manual Based on The Tibetan Book of the Dead is an instruction manual intended to serve as a model and a guide for all subsequent mind-expanding inquiries involving psychedelic drugs.
Co-authored by Timothy Leary, Ralph Metzner, and Richard Alpert, the fathers of psychedelia, *The Psychedelic Experience*, published in 1964, describes their discoveries in broadening spiritual consciousness through a combination of Tibetan meditation techniques and psychotropic substances.

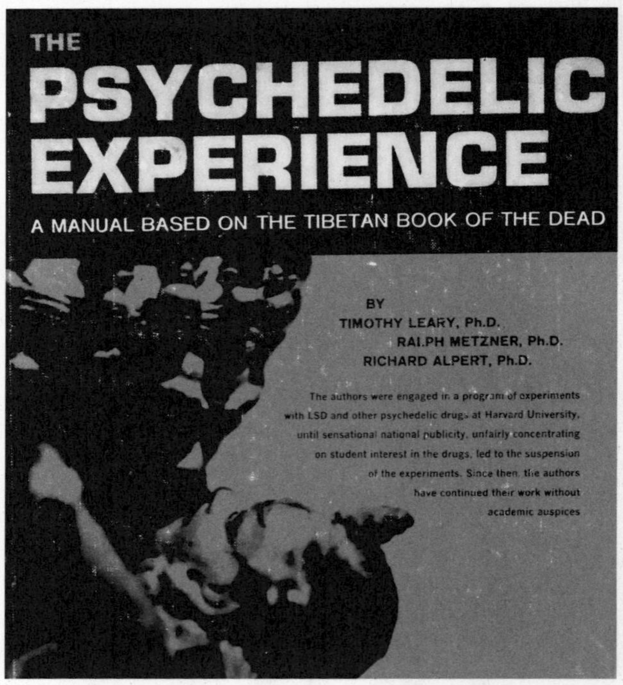

Cover for the first edition of *The Psychedelic Experience. A Manual Based on the Tibetan Book of the Dead*, by Timothy Leary, Ralph Metzner, and Richard Alpert, 1964

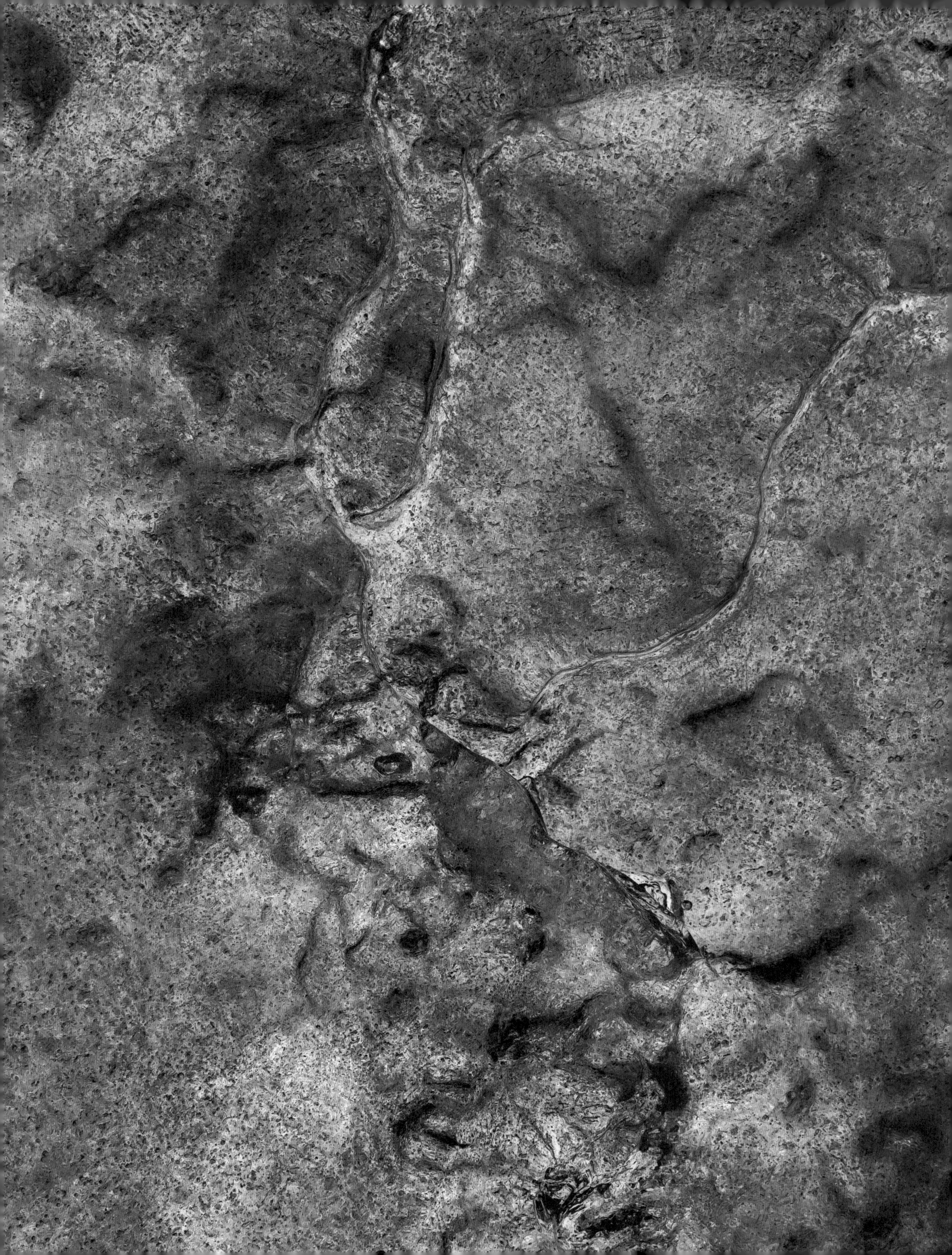